Adding English
Helping English Language Learners
Succeed in School

by
Katherine Maitland

Good Apple

DEDICATION

To my parents Fred and Lois Maitland,
who brought me up bilingual.

ACKNOWLEDGMENTS

Many thanks to the following persons for their time and helpful
suggestions: Karen Gilbert, Melissa Linnick, Lois Maitland,
Jeanne Piña, and Mary Lynn Thomson.

With special thanks to my husband, Barry McGhan, who provided
invaluable technical assistance and emotional support.

SENIOR EDITOR
Susan Eddy

EDITOR
Alexandra Behr

INTERIOR DESIGNER
Lisa Ann Arcuri

COVER PHOTOGRAPHER
John Paul Endress

GOOD APPLE
A Division of Frank Schaffer Publication, Inc.
23740 Hawthorne Boulevard
Torrance, CA 90505-5927

3 4 5 6 7 8 9 MAL 01 00 99 98

Contents

Introduction

Growing up in Brazil as the child of American parents, I lived between two worlds—two languages and two cultures. In the process of making sense of these worlds, I built my own.

Although I understood and spoke English, adjusting to American culture at the age of 16 was still a scary and difficult process. Moving between two worlds created moments of exhilaration and of deep ambivalence. As an adult, I was drawn to issues of language learning, bilingualism, and acculturation.

Adding English: Helping English Language Learners Succeed in School describes many challenges facing a student who is trying to function in school and negotiate a new language and culture. For every person the journey entails different twists and turns.

ESL students long to be seen as capable people. They yearn for someone who can appreciate them as unique individuals, beyond the barriers of language. Like other students, they arrive with language, culture, and history.

Students should feel whole and secure, part of the classroom community. Only then will they gain the greatest educational benefit from their school experiences. Too often a school's message to cross-cultural students is: "Put aside your culture and language so you can learn English." If we ask them to leave their first language and culture outside the classroom door, they feel unaccepted, and their progress is slowed.

There is a cost to pay if we view students as deficient, needing to replace their home language with English. Pressured by their surroundings and searching for acceptance, students do give up their first language. When this happens, it often disrupts family life. If English replaces the home language, parents and grandparents may lose their ability to fully communicate with their children.

Although adults may want to learn English, their command of the language is often faulty and less robust than their primary language. Students who use only English with their parents lose opportunities to develop deeper levels of language.

We need to invite students to add English to their rich repertoire of language and experiences. And we need to learn from them. When students sense acceptance at school, they participate more willingly. They see themselves as contributors, not just members who must "fit in." If we create a community that encourages social interaction where everyone benefits, learning will take place.

Adding English is a simple and practical handbook to guide teachers in helping students who are acquiring English. Learning an additional language is a complex process, affected by many factors. In a few places, I have used examples from my students to illustrate certain points. These are composite portraits; students' names, ages, and countries of origin have been changed.

I have tried to avoid using the terms *limited English proficient (LEP)* and *language minority student*, because they promote a connotation of inadequacy. (*LEP* is used later in the introduction, however, in references to government statistics.) At times I refer to *cross-cultural students* (Clayton, 1996). This term emphasizes the process of acculturation that is part of negotiating a new environment. I have also relied on terms such as *English as a second language (ESL)*, *English language learner (ELL)*, and *second-language learner*, realizing, of course, that English is a third or fourth language for some students.

Statistics show that English language learners come from around the world. In some cases their families come to the U.S. temporarily because of schooling or employment. Students' American schooling, though brief, may become a significant portion of their childhood. Other families are refugees from war-torn countries or have fled intolerable political or economic situations. Still other students were born in the U.S., but come from homes where English is not the primary language.

Some students come from families with means. They can afford tutoring, computers, and other material goods that make the transition between cultures easier. Others arrive with only the desire and determination to make better lives for themselves.

No matter what the circumstances, these families send their children to schools expecting that they will learn. ESL students deserve to be seen as capable learners. They deserve opportunities within the school community to add English to their lives and world views.

The Big Picture

Immigration is an integral part of our nation's history. In the 1980s the U.S. witnessed the largest influx of immigrants ever. About 9.5 million people came to our shores (Liu, 1994).

How many U.S. residents speak a language other than English?

According to the 1990 U.S. Census, almost 32 million people speak languages other than English in their homes.

What are some of the languages spoken by the limited English proficient (LEP) student population?

LEP Student Population Distribution by Language 1991-1992 School Year		
Language Goup	Number of LEP Students	Percentage of LEP Students
Spanish	1,682,560	72.9
Vietnamese	90,922	3.9
Hmong	42,305	1.8
Cantonese	38,693	1.7
Cambodian	37,742	1.6
Korean	36,568	1.6
Laotian	29,838	1.3
Navajo	28,913	1.3
Tagalog	24,516	1.1
Russian	21,903	0.9
Creole (French)	21,850	0.9
Arabic	20,318	0.9
Portuguese	15,298	0.7
Japanese	13,913	0.6
Armenian	11,916	0.5
Chinese (unspec.)	11,540	0.5
Mandarin	11,020	0.5
Farsi	8,563	0.4
Hindi	7,905	0.3
Polish	6,747	0.3

The number of Hispanic students in the U.S. continues to soar—12 million in 1996, up from 9.8 million in 1990. By 2040 Hispanic children will constitute an estimated 25% of the preschool population (Jones, 1996).

How many LEP students attend schools?

The government estimates that nearly 2.3 million LEP students attended K–12 public schools from 1990–91 (Source: NCBE Forum, 1993). By the 1993–94 school year, about 2.7 million LEP students were enrolled in schools (Source: Development Associates, 1995).

Do all LEP students receive bilingual or ESL services?

No. Nearly a half-million LEP students (about 17.6% of all LEP students) were not in any special programs in 1994 (Source: Development Associates, 1995).

Does speaking a language other than English in the home mean that students will grow up limited in English?

No. Students can grow up learning more than one language simultaneously. Some individuals become "coordinate bilinguals," equally proficient in two languages.

CHAPTER 1

Second-Language Acquisition

A Process, Not an Event

- LEARNING A LANGUAGE IS LIKE A ROLLER-COASTER RIDE, FILLED WITH HIGHS AND LOWS, DIZZYING TWISTS AND TURNS.

- LEARNING A LANGUAGE IS LIKE GOING ON A JOURNEY. THE PATH IS NEW TERRAIN, FILLED WITH SURPRISES.

- LEARNING A LANGUAGE IS LIKE BECOMING A NEW PERSON. YOU TRY NEW WAYS OF BEHAVING. SOMETIMES IT IS COMFORTABLE; SOMETIMES IT IS NOT.

When students learn a second language they use everything they have—their first language, culture, cognitive knowledge, and personal experiences—to interact with the new environment. In the process of this "creative construction" (Dulay and others, 1982), they slowly organize and refine rules for the new language system.

What they must refine, however, is not just a knowledge of grammar, but a complex interplay of elements, including the abilities to choose ways of saying things; to use the functions of language, such as arguing, complaining, and apologizing; to say things appropriately in social contexts; and to use strategies when communication breaks down.

Students acquire a second language when they receive an understandable message. If the language contains structures that are only slightly beyond their level, they take in "comprehensible input" (Krashen, 1985). One more condition, however, is essential for language acquisition. The learner must be open to it—free from too much anxiety or fear of failure.

To help our students succeed in school, we need to provide English-language learners with access to comprehensible input. We must strive to create nonthreatening environments for the entire school day, including lunch, bus time, and assemblies.

Felipe is an outgoing second grader who loves to talk with friends. His teacher is puzzled because Felipe can speak English, yet is making very slow progress in reading and other content areas. Why, she wonders, can't he "get" it? Is he just being stubborn?

Students like Felipe have mastered face-to-face conversational skills. Their interactions depend on cues—facial expressions, gestures, the context of the situation, and the tone of voice. When language becomes more abstract, such as in academic settings, comprehension diminishes. Without support, many ESL students flounder when asked to negotiate more cognitively challenging tasks.

English-language learners may pick up conversational English, or basic interpersonal communicative skills (BICS), within two years. School language, or cognitive academic language proficiency (CALPS), may take five to seven years, or even longer (Collier, 1987; Cummins, 1984).

What Affects Language Acquisition?

Yuki arrived in the U.S. two years ago. She was placed in a fourth-grade classroom where there were no other Japanese students. Shy and reserved, Yuki did not initiate conversations, nor did she volunteer answers in class. During recess, Yuki chose to play with Japanese girls from other rooms.

Since the classroom teacher felt that Yuki could not read or write until she could speak English, Yuki was not expected to do much of her classwork. The only exception was mastery of a spelling book one grade level below her class. For the rest of the day, Yuki was on her own: She determined what she could and could not accomplish. Nevertheless, Yuki was one of the top students in math. Only the language-based problems troubled her.

By the end of the school year, Yuki had made disappointing progress in English. Because few of the assignments had been adapted for her, she had little experience in handling academic English. Low expectations from the teacher and little support for language acquisition kept her from making much progress.

As Yuki's story shows, simply being placed in an English-speaking environment isn't enough to guarantee language acquisition and academic growth. During this time of transition, students need guidance and support. Yuki, however, was unable to seek help in class, something most American teachers expect from their students. The teacher thought she was doing Yuki a favor by waiting for her oral skills to emerge. This strategy cut her off from much that was taking place in the classroom.

All too often, a student's parents are struggling with their cultural adjustment and can't give her what she needs. It is crucial, therefore, for teachers to work with parents to help support the student during this period of adjustment.

For most students who move between cultures, the question "Who will be my friend?" is central in their adjusting to school. Yuki sought the comfort of students from her country. Although these friendships helped buffer culture shock, her dependence on them kept her from taking more risks in English. And Yuki's shyness kept her from much-needed interaction with English-speaking students.

Clayton (1996: 68) writes about cross-cultural students who are adjusting to U.S. classrooms: "For the gregarious students, learning the language meant more friends, which, in turn, meant learning the language faster. For shy students, the spiral slowed and almost degenerated as language developed at a much slower pace."

Learning a second language is a complex, multifaceted process that can be affected by many factors. The following chart shows some of these variables.

Factors Affecting Second-Language Acquisition

Factors in the Student	Age
	Proficiency in home language
	Literacy in home language
	Cognitive development in home language
	Maintenance of home language
	Date of arrival
	Reason for coming to U.S.
	Stage in acculturation
	Personality
	Motivation
	Family support
	Sense of identity within classroom
	Learning style
Factors in the Family	Literacy level
	Facility with English and ability to help child
	Socioeconomic status
	Attitudes toward second culture
	Expectations for child
	Projected length of stay
Factors Related to the Environment of the Second Culture	Culture of classroom
	Teacher's expectations
	How host culture views student's culture
	Whether environment provides adequate "input"
	Role models
	Whether student has enough opportunities to use English
	Whether school environment allows for adequate language usage

The Role of Culture

Culture is a complex system of patterns of behavior, comprising the "total way of life of particular groups of people" (Kohls, 1996: 23). Culture is passed down from generation to generation, evolving with each and rooting itself deeply in the consciousness of individuals. The following web shows some important components of cultures.

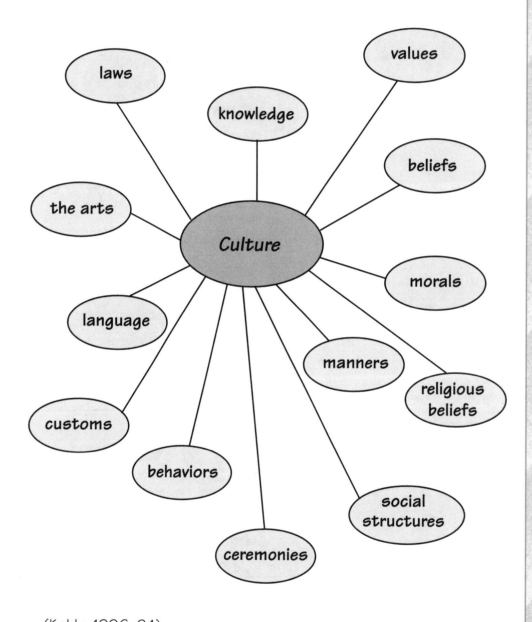

(Kohls, 1996: 24)

Cultural Perceptions

If you ask a Brazilian what his first perceptions of Americans are, he might say, "The people here seem friendly at first, but they are really quite reserved, not open like Brazilians." If you ask someone from Japan the same question, she may say, "Americans are so friendly and outgoing!"

Which view of Americans is accurate? Both have validity because cultural perceptions are *relative*. Observations, impressions, and conclusions depend on one's background. We can talk more knowledgeably about cultural differences by first knowing something specific about our culture.

On the surface this seems like an easy assignment . . . but is it really? According to anthropologist Edward T. Hall (1959: 30), "Culture hides much more than it reveals, and strangely enough what it hides, it hides most effectively from its participants."

Culture defines who we are and how we think. Like fish in water, we are surrounded by culture. Stepping back and identifying aspects of our culture is difficult. Most often, we are not aware of deeply held values. We do not come face to face with them until a contrasting view arises. Even then, we may not perceive the source of our unease or discomfort. We see our way as "right" rather than "different." This is true not only of us, but also of ESL students and their families.

We will be better equipped to help students make the necessary cross-cultural adjustments if we can become aware of some differences and suspend judgments about others. We cannot control how others will feel and act, but we can manage our behavior through a conscious effort to learn about cultural diversity.

Attributes of American Culture

This topic is somewhat difficult to address because we are a nation of immigrants. Even so, some basic patterns of behavior, values, and assumptions can be drawn about American life.

Individualism How would you respond to this statement: "People have to realize that they can only count on their own skills and abilities if they're going to win in this world." According to a 1995 *Time* magazine poll, 86% of respondents agreed with the statement (Hull, 1995).

At the core of American identity is the concept of individualism and self-reliance. We derive most of our sense of self not from which group we belong to, or which ancestral family we come from, but the identity we have forged for ourselves.

Equality Although reflected unevenly in practice, the notion that all humans are created equal is deeply rooted. For Americans, people are born with equal worth and deserve respect because they are human beings.

Egalitarian behavior may puzzle some internationals who rely on titles of honor and deferential treatment to show respect. Most Americans feel uncomfortable with such customs, but fail to notice that we too have ways of showing respect for persons in higher stations. For example, we allow our superiors at work to speak first and for longer periods, give them special parking privileges, and defer to their decisions.

Informality We like to use first names, dress casually, and speak informally. This apparent lack of rules of behavior may be disorienting to persons who come from more traditional or formal cultures.

Achievement When meeting a new acquaintance, one of the first things Americans ask is, "What do you do for a living?" Our society is action- and achievement-oriented. We admire those who get things done. Hard work is respected, and from this follows a pursuit of material things. Big houses and big cars are hallmarks of success.

People in other parts of the world work hard, too. Yet, work may play a less central role in their identities. Spending time with family and friends may be an integral part of their lives. "We work to live, and you live to work!" some internationals say.

How American Cultural Values Affect Students

Students who come from cultures that affirm *group* identity may have trouble adjusting to an environment that highlights individualism. Making choices and decisions, performing self-assessments, working independently, and relying on individual efforts to "make the grade" may create uncomfortable expectations. Cross-cultural students need time to adjust to new ways. They need someone to explain expectations and give guidance in learning these new behaviors.

A related area that presents problems is the degree of responsibility expected of students. In some cultures young students are not expected to be independent. Adults supervise, monitor, and do more for them. Thus, some parents may feel American teachers expect too much from their child, and they may want the teachers to offer more help.

American classrooms are often run in a manner that reflects the informality of the majority culture. For example, students do not usually stand to address the teacher. They interact in a casual manner with their classmates and staff members. This lack of formality does not mean a lack of rules. But it does mean that students who come from an environment in which there are highly structured expectations for behavior may have difficulty understanding what is expected of them. They may have a vague sense of unease that there is a lack of authority and lack of respect between students and teachers.

Conversely, students from other cultures may feel there is too much social distance between teachers and students. They cannot call their teacher "Auntie." They cannot even show respect by calling her "Teacher," because Americans insist on being called by their names. And why, they wonder, doesn't the teacher use language that demonstrates warmth and affection? Styles of communication that are different may disorient students. Something is "off," but they are unable to say what it is.

The concept of time is also culturally bound. In the U.S., where bells ring and where people live by appointments and schedules, time is compartmentalized, counted, and controlled. Fifteen minutes spent on spelling, a half-hour on math, and twenty-five minutes on reading may seem unnatural to some students and parents, especially when there is little or no transition time between activities.

Finally, most Americans strive to maintain positive interactions with others. We believe an upbeat tone enhances communication. It is no surprise that most U.S. teachers will begin report cards or parent-teacher conferences with positive comments and a list of student strengths. This style of communication may be unfamiliar and even confusing to ESL parents and students, who expect a more straightforward manner of addressing concerns. It may be a good idea to prepare parents by explaining what you would like to do during your time together.

MANAGING CULTURAL DIFFERENCES

- Accept that there are *different* ways, not right or wrong ways.

- Maintain a sense of humor.

- Use bilingual and bicultural members of the community as cultural interpreters.

- Learn about American culture—its values and assumptions.

- Learn about your students' cultures.

Adjusting to a New Culture

There are many ways students handle their new American culture. The "Withdrawn Student" becomes sullen and quiet. Because her landscape has changed so drastically, she grieves her losses, maybe even her sense of lost identity. The "Compliant Student" conforms quickly to her new environment and, like a chameleon, changes colors. This type of behavior may create disturbances at home, where a family becomes alarmed and wonders what happened to the child they no longer recognize.

Still others can be characterized as the "Well-Adjusted Student." They find strategies to make more balanced cross-cultural adjustments. They neither reject nor comply, but find a middle ground. They retain a strong sense of self, while accepting and accommodating new ways of thinking and behaving. They achieve equilibrium and can move easily between the home culture and school.

Adults and older students may find some comfort in knowing that most people who cross cultures go through predictable phases. The intensity and duration of each phase will vary according to the individual's personality and circumstances.

The first phase is usually brief and is characterized by excitement. Like a tourist snapping photos at every fascinating new sight, a newcomer is in a state of euphoria. Soon, however, the excitement wears off and is replaced with a sense of uneasiness. The newcomer may fall into a slump. Besieged by all the new things—from gestures to language to social customs—he enters a stage of culture shock and begins to see the negative aspects of the new environment. The energy needed to cope with the strangeness of customs and language fatigues the newcomer. He may feel homesick, irritable, worried, fearful, or hostile.

Gradually, the newcomer begins to find strategies for adjusting to the environment. The differences are still there, but they are less of a problem. He regains a sense of confidence and begins to negotiate the new landscape. Given time, patience, and motivation, he eventually becomes more comfortable in his new culture.

Symptoms of Culture Shock	
General	Specific
anxiety	inability to concentrate
homesickness	withdrawing from others
fatigue	irritability
crying	tendency to fight or argue
illness	feeling superior to others
depression	feeling inferior to others
(Kohls, 1996: 92)	

TIPS ON WEATHERING CULTURE SHOCK

You may wish to share these ideas with families.

- Let your child know that ambivalent feelings—or even negative ones—are a normal part of adjusting to a new culture.

- Take time to have fun with your child.

- Make sure there is time to relax.

- Take time to use the home language.

- Find other families who are also adjusting to American culture.

- Avoid criticizing the new culture too much.

- Maintain a sense of humor.

- Make sure your child gets enough rest.

- Seek medical help when needed.

Chapter 2

Helping Students Add English

First Days

Cross-cultural students often experience a period of vulnerability during the first few days in school. Their emotions might encompass fearfulness and uncertainty as well as excitement and high expectations. A welcoming environment will assure families that we are sensitive to their needs. The following suggestions will help students make a smoother transition.

School Tour Allow parents and students an opportunity to visit the school before students' first full day. Volunteers, administrators, or other school personnel can lead a guided tour of the school building. They might describe the school's special programs or features and some of the expectations. If parents do not speak English, enlist bilingual volunteers to help with communication.

School Handbook Provide a handbook that lists information about school policies, programs, personnel, and emergency procedures. If these materials are not available in the family's home language, ask bilingual volunteers to interpret and answer questions. The parents should also furnish the names and phone numbers of bilingual neighbors or friends to contact during an emergency.

Having the right shoes for gym class, bringing a book to read during silent reading, and knowing about special computer classes may seem like insignificant details to adults. Yet cross-cultural students are navigating unknown territory. They already feel different because of their language and appearance. Being prepared for the "small" things helps them relax and feel more in control.

What Parents Should Know

- How the student should address the teacher
- School lunch routines
- Special routines, such as silent reading
- Schedules for library and special classes
- Required supplies and clothing, such as gym shoes
- Recess
- Snacks
- Bus routines

Buddy System Pairing an English learner with a classmate will make the transition smoother. When assigning buddies, ask for volunteers. Students who speak the same language may not necessarily make the best partners. They may have varying degrees of facility with their home language, and some may have difficulty translating. Others may feel embarrassed to be singled out. The system is more successful when students choose to help others. However, helpers often view their task as a burden after the initial excitement wears off. Be sensitive to this arrangement and reassign partners periodically.

Classroom Conduct Coach classmates on how to help the newcomer. Discuss with students what it means to learn a new language and how it feels to be in a new environment. Your attitudes and actions will influence how students treat English-language learners. Small things you do in the first weeks can make their lives a little easier. If necessary, point out the following.

- Non-English speakers are not "slow." They already speak a language and function well in their culture.

- Newcomers have many interesting experiences, skills, and knowledge to share with the class. The learning can be mutually rewarding.

- Learning a language means making lots of mistakes. Patience and encouragement will help new students acquire English. It is *unacceptable* to laugh at students' attempts to learn English.

- Newcomers will feel welcome when they are included in classroom and playground activities.

Other Tips

Give English learners frequent breaks. Listening to and trying to understand a new language can be exhausting. After a while, English learners tune out. This may be self-preservation more than anything else. It does not mean they are deliberately ignoring you or refusing to try. Do not force students to speak or repeat words before they are ready. They can respond with nonverbal gestures, such as shaking their heads.

As soon as possible, give newcomers routine tasks that are regularly assigned to classmates. This will give them a sense of belonging. English learners can participate in activities that are not heavily dependent on language. Make it clear that you expect them to take part, and support them in the process.

Often, English learners will mimic what others are doing. Although this is one strategy for learning, it can trick you and others into thinking they understand what they are doing and why. You will need to make frequent checks for comprehension.

Hearing verbal directions will not be enough for students learning English. They will need demonstrations of what you mean. Break down complicated assignments into easier steps and have students role-play class procedures and tasks.

Meeting With Parents

Students from other cultures may have had quite different experiences in schooling. To better understand your students and their needs, try to learn about their backgrounds. The following questions may help you develop a list to use during parent-teacher conferences. If necessary, have a bilingual interpreter assist with communication.

Questions to Ask Parents

- How do students address their teachers in your country? (Explain that most teachers in the United States prefer to be called by their names.)

- How formal was your child's previous schooling? (What was the child's relationship to the teacher? to other students? How were lessons conducted? For example, did students stand to recite their lessons?)

- How much responsibility did your child have for completing classwork and homework assignments, staying on task, and monitoring progress?

- What subjects did your child study most recently in school?

- Was your child doing well in math? in reading? What grades did she or he receive?

- How did your child see her or his abilities at school?

- Which school activities does your child enjoy?

- Did your child work in small groups, or is she or he used to a teacher lecturing?

- Do you understand the curriculum in this school?

- What questions do you have?

The following questions and concerns that parents might ask can arise out of differing cultural perspectives about what happens—or should happen—in schools. Their questions will depend on their cultural perspective and experiences.

Questions Parents May Ask

- What are the rules of the school? How will my child know what to do?

- Why is there so little respect for adults and for education? Why are students allowed to eat in class? Why do teachers sit on their desks?

- Why are students moving around the room so much? Why aren't they reciting their lessons?

- Why doesn't my child bring her textbooks home every day? Why don't you have textbooks for all the subjects?

- Why doesn't my child have more homework?

- Why are there so many strict schedules (25 minutes for science, 15 minutes for silent reading, and so on)?

- Why is my child expected to do so much for herself?

- Why doesn't the teacher remind my child about homework assignments and tests?

- Why doesn't the teacher help my child on a one-to-one basis more often?

- Why doesn't the teacher communicate with me more often about my child?

Home Languages in the Classroom

A student's first language is an integral part of her or his identity. It is a strength and asset, to be built upon and added to. Embracing students' home culture and language in appropriate and meaningful ways affirms their identity and develops self-confidence. Such positive attitudes demonstrate that we can learn from others, too. A warm and accepting climate invites students to add English to their lives.

Promoting the use of native languages offers academic benefits. Classmates and teachers will view English learners as capable students when they are given a chance to demonstrate their abilities. In turn, students begin to see themselves as readers and writers, taking more risks in English (Hudelson, 1987).

Many researchers believe that developing cognitive and academic skills in students' native languages helps support learning in English. Bilingual students develop a "common underlying proficiency," which can be used as a resource in either language (Cummins, 1981). The languages share an underlying base and are not entirely separate. A firm cognitive rooting in students' native languages will support them as they develop skills in English.

Promoting Home Languages

How are we to promote a home language when our classrooms reflect many languages, or when we are monolingual? The following suggestions can help you accept home cultures and languages in ways that promote respect and self-confidence and develop academic skills.

- Invite bilingual parents and community volunteers to participate in classroom activities. They might lead small-group discussions, read material written in native languages, teach songs, or share information.

- Have students work with bilingual tutors or parents to create posters and charts in their home languages. Suggest topics such as number words, color words, alphabet charts, and welcome signs. Ask cooperative groups to make posters of key words in several languages.

- Invite students to share books written in their home languages. They may also teach the class greetings, counting, and simple phrases. Let the class learn and sing songs, such as "Happy Birthday," in other languages.

- Encourage parents to maintain their native language in the home. Never insist that parents speak only English to their children. If appropriate, send class materials home to be explained in the native language.

- Provide as many materials written in native languages as possible—books, magazines, videos, and computer software. Bilingual community volunteers or school aides can work with students using these resources.

David and Yvonne Freeman (1992) developed the following helpful suggestions for teachers who do not speak students' language.

- Have students write pen-pal letters in their native languages to students in other schools.

- Build a library of home-language materials. If necessary, pool resources with other teachers.

- Invite each student to use his or her primary language in journal writing. Bilingual parents or tutors can work with students and write responses.

- Collect ESL students' writings in their home languages and print copies of them to add to the classroom library. Invite students to share their stories.

Classroom Techniques

"Comprehensible input" is the language that students understand through the context of a situation. The environment, the speaker's use of gestures and facial expressions, and other visual cues all contribute. Since the language is slightly beyond the student's level, he or she must be relaxed and comfortable to "take in" the language.

There are many ways to adjust our instruction to provide students with comprehensible input. These include not only the language we use, but also the classroom climate and management. Wong-Fillmore (1985) describes the following tactics.

- Provide signals to call students' attention to different lessons. Use such techniques as the location of the lesson, teacher posture, voice cues, and predictable schedules to mark the lesson's boundaries.

- Build consistency in classroom routines, lesson formats, and the language used within lessons. Familiarity with procedures frees English learners to concentrate on content.

- Provide a balance between teacher-centered instruction and independent work. Too much individual work will deprive students of necessary social interaction.

- Use students' feedback to adapt instruction and assignments. With beginners, elicit responses through short-answer questions. At the same time, encourage students to stretch beyond their comfort level. Give them opportunities to hear and use slightly more complex language.

- Repeat, rephrase, paraphrase, and expand. Focus on communication!

- Use powerful, evocative, or playful language. Make language memorable for students.

MEANING is negotiated between you and the learner. As the student gives you feedback, adjust your language to ensure your communication conveys your intended message.

Above all, we should make activities meaningful and purposeful. Much of language learning and conceptual understanding develops through social interactions within the classroom.

The following techniques and resources will help make language more accessible to English learners.

- Use your whole body to convey what you mean. Gestures, skipping, crouching, and other body motions clarify what you say. Facial expressions convey emotions and emphasize the message. Frequent pauses help you check for comprehension and allow students to process language. Your voice (tone, volume, and intonation) reinforces what you want to express.

- Provide visual cues. Make quick sketches on the chalkboard. Use real objects and models, such as plastic fruit. Display photographs, pictures, charts, and posters. Use filmstrips, videos, and computer programs with graphics.

- Encourage student interactions in different combinations and for a variety of purposes. Have students work with partners or in small collaborative groups. Develop plans for conversations, sharing, and interviews.

- Use demonstrations followed by students working in cooperative groups as an integral part of instruction. Include demonstrations in cooking activities, art activities, science experiments, building or making items, and writing or speaking activities.

- Dramatizations make complex language more explicit. Act out fingerplays, songs, and stories. Role-play situations. Dramatize selections from long stories or novels.

- Make classroom routines and procedures predictable. Make sure students understand the key words used in giving directions. Help students know what is expected and what comes next to give them a sense of confidence. Use predictable routines and activities to free students to concentrate on understanding content.

It is not enough to provide stand-alone activities. To internalize language, students need to hear it and use it many times and in many ways. Thus, we need to recycle concepts, revisit stories and songs, and connect them to other activities.

We can read a story and act it out, invite students to respond by painting a picture, or sing a related song. We can have the class observe an animal, write a language-experience story, and then read a related nonfiction book. In so doing, we weave a fabric of activities that allows students to learn content and to use language for a variety of purposes.

Using Visuals to Support Language Learning

ESL students need lots of visual clues. You already use many of the suggestions that follow. The difference is in the degree and frequency that you employ these materials to help ESL students. You will find that many students will benefit from the increased visual support.

Concrete Objects The feel, smell, and look of real objects is often the best way to observe and learn about the world. Talking about and looking at pictures of fruits may be fun, but how much more exciting to touch, feel, and taste real fruit! The use of the senses makes language memorable, and thus the use of real objects is indispensable in language learning.

Realia These are objects that represent the "real thing." Empty boxes of cereal, for example, show what you are talking about when you study nutrition. Your grade level, classroom budget, and storage space will influence the types of materials you use. You may wish to borrow materials from preschool and kindergarten classrooms.

Pictures and Photos A picture file is essential in working with English-language learners. Pictures can be used and reused in dozens of ways to aid comprehension. Invite students to find pictures for you. For example, have them scour magazines for images of people, then help them categorize the pictures as families, children, or workers. If possible, students can work with family members to collect multicultural pictures from magazines at home.

Graphs These convey information visually and make academic language more explicit. Graphs that students create from their experiences are the most useful, since the graphs express what they have observed.

Charts and Diagrams Charts can be printed posters or ones that you or your students create. They are especially helpful in illustrating a process, such as the water cycle. Make sure they are clearly labeled and illustrated at the appropriate level for your language learners.

Charts in Progress You and your class create these charts as learning unfolds. For example, as students study parts of a fish, they may add more labels to the chart. Or, you may have a list of words that describe character traits. Throughout the semester, students may add new words. As the chart grows, you may engage students in a variety of activities, such as drawing a character from a story, pantomiming given words, or classifying the words.

Contrasting Charts Contrasting charts can help students make cross-cultural connections. For example, if you are studying plants, one group of students can create charts showing types of local trees. Other groups can research and develop charts of trees found in other regions of the U.S. or the world.

Displays These make use of real objects and realia. If appropriate, encourage students to bring items from home to display. Have them work with you to add labels. Displays can give bilingual tutors or teachers' aides a context with which to work with students. Displays can also be used for informal assessments.

For example, remove labels from a display and ask students to match the objects in the display with the labels.

Collections As you develop curriculum-based classroom materials, ask students to help you create permanent or temporary collections. For example, if you are studying the ocean, have students work with family members to collect shells.

Models These are useful tools for English learners because they represent real life. Students can work individually or cooperatively to put together models. The hands-on approach will engage them in purposeful language.

Life Maps and Time Lines These activities give students visual clues to abstract concepts, such as chronological events and the lives of individuals. Encourage students to illustrate milestones. More advanced students can write text as well.

Reading Aloud

Reading aloud to students is one of the best ways to help bridge the gap between conversational English and academic language skills. Reading aloud is an invitation for students to join what Smith (1983) calls the "literacy club."

When you read to your class you are expressing your love and enjoyment of reading. You are unleashing the transforming power of the printed word. You are providing comprehensible input and building students' knowledge base. You are opening new doors—linguistic, cultural, cognitive, and emotional—to each student's world.

The language of literature is complex and rich. It may be playful, using humor that reflects cultural nuances. Or it may be filled with imagery. Students who are learning English as a second language need to hear such pieces. At the same time, however, the language may be very challenging.

Beginning and intermediate ESL students will need books that support the listener. Illustrations should help students make sense of the text. The text should be simple—not too far above a student's language level. Avoid texts that rely too heavily on idiomatic expressions, colloquialisms, and dialect. The story should contain strong elements for its genre: plot, characters, predictable pattern, or suspense.

What you do with literature will also affect how much students "get" from it. Following a three-step approach to reading aloud will enhance language acquisition.

1. **Before Reading** Prepare students for the story. Share your enthusiasm for the book and tell them why you like it. Show students the book's cover, and have them predict what it is about. Tap students' prior knowledge by asking them questions and brainstorming ideas. Invite them to tell about personal experiences related to the topic.

2. **During Reading** While sharing the book, make the reading as dramatic as possible! Read the story in a clear and slow pace. Use your voice—tone, volume, stress, and intonation—to emphasize meaning. Pause to allow students to process what they are hearing.

3. **After Reading** Provide follow-up activities. Students need to act on what they have heard. These activities may help them build comprehension, extend language, and make connections. They also help you assess what students have learned.

   - Let students act out the story through pantomime or drama. Use puppets, character masks, and other props to make the dramatizations come alive.

   - With beginners, ask questions that require yes-or-no or one-word answers. More experienced students can handle short-answer and open-ended questions.

   - With the class, complete a graphic organizer, such as a story map or a chart that lists character traits. You may wish to let students illustrate the chart.

Character	What the Character Is Like	How Do We Know?
Little Willy in *Stone Fox*	Determined	Doc Smith and the banker tell him to give up, but he doesn't. Willy and Searchlight dig up all the potatoes.

- Compare the book with other stories you have read to the class. Again, graphic organizers and artwork help with this process.

- Nonverbal responses give English learners an opportunity to demonstrate their understanding. Some students may wish to respond through art—a means of self-expression that is not limited by language constraints. Ask students to draw a favorite part of the story or a favorite character. Have students sketch the most exciting part of the story, or make puppets and props for a dramatization. Invite students to draw or paint what will happen next.

Read-Aloud Books
Multicultural

Adler, David. **The Picture Book of Martin Luther King, Jr.** Holiday House, 1989.

Baer, Edith. **This Is the Way We Go to School: A Book About Students Around the World.** Scholastic, 1990.

Delacre, Lulu. **Vejigante.** Scholastic, 1993.

Feelings, Muriel. **Moja Means One: Swahili Counting Book.** Dial, 1971.

Feelings, Muriel. **Jambo Means Hello: Swahili Alphabet Book.** Dial, 1974.

Goble, Paul. **Buffalo Woman.** Bradbury, 1984.

Griego, Margot and others. **Tortillitas Para Mama and Other Nursery Rhymes: Spanish & English.** Holt, 1981.

Grossman, Virginia and Sylvia Long. **Ten Little Rabbits.** Chronicle Books, 1991.

Haskins, Jim. **Count Your Way Through the Arab World.** Carolrhoda, 1987.

Heide, Florence Parry and Judith Heide. **The Day of Ahmed's Secret.** Lothrop, Lee & Shepard, 1990.

Johnson, Angela. **Tell Me a Story, Mama.** Franklin Watts, 1989.

Knight, Margy Burns. **Talking Walls.** Tilbury House, 1992.

Lessac, Frané. **My Little Island.** Lippincott, 1985.

Lewin, Ted. **Market!** Lothrop, Lee & Shepard, 1996.

McDermott, Gerald. **Anansi the Spider.** Holt, 1972.

McDermott, Gerald. **Arrow to the Sun: A Pueblo Indian Tale.** Viking Press, 1974.

Martin, Bill, Jr. **I Am Freedom's Child.** DLM Teaching Resources, 1987.

Morris, Ann. **Loving.** Scholastic, 1990.

Morris, Ann. **Hats, Hats, Hats.** Lothrop, Lee & Shepard, 1989.

Morris, Ann. **Bread, Bread, Bread.** Macmillan/McGraw-Hill, 1989.

Papi, Liza. *Carnavalia! African-Brazilian Folklore and Crafts.* Rizzoli, 1994.

Rossman, Virginia and Sylvia Long. *Ten Little Rabbits.* Chronicle Books, 1991.

Surat, Michelle Maria. *Angel Child, Dragon Child.* Raintree, 1983.

Waters, Kate and Madeline Slovanz-Low. *Lion Dancer.* Scholastic, 1990.

Williams, Vera. *A Chair for My Mother.* Greenwillow, 1982.

Yashima, Taro. *Umbrella.* Puffin, 1958.

Young, Ed. *Lon Po-Po: A Red Riding Hood Story from China.* Philomel, 1989.

Pattern Books

Brown, Ruth. *A Dark, Dark Tale.* Dial, 1981.

Christelow, Eileen. *Five Little Monkeys Jumping on the Bed.* Clarion, 1989.

Cowley, Joy. *Mrs. Wishy-Washy.* The Wright Group, 1980.

Emberley, Barbara. *Drummer Hoff.* Prentice-Hall, 1967.

Flack, Marjorie. *Ask Mr. Bear.* Macmillan, 1932.

Martin, Bill, Jr. *Brown Bear, Brown Bear, What Do You See?* Henry Holt, 1983.

Numeroff, Lara Joffe. *If You Give a Mouse a Cookie.* Harper & Row, 1985.

Rosen, Michael and Helen Oxenbury. *We're Going on a Bear Hunt.* Margaret K. McElderry, 1989.

Shaw, Charles G. *It Looked Like Spilt Milk.* Harper & Row, 1947.

Tetherington, Jeanette. *Pumpkin, Pumpkin.* Greenwillow, 1986.

Ward, Leila. *I Am Eyes: Ni Macho.* Scholastic, 1978.

Ward, Cindy. *Cookie's Week.* G.P. Putnam, 1988.

West, Colin. *"Pardon?" said the Giraffe.* Lippincott, 1986.

Wildsmith, Brian. *Toot Toot.* Oxford University Press, 1989.

Wordless (or near)

Briggs, Raymond. *Snowman.* Random House, 1978.

Florian, Douglas. *Airplane Ride.* Crowell, 1984.

Hoban, Tana. *Is It Red? Is It Yellow? Is It Blue?* Mulberry Books, 1978.

Hutchins, Pat. *Changes, Changes.* Macmillan, 1971.

McCully, Emily Arnold. *School.* Trumpet Club, 1991.

McCully, Emily Arnold. *First Snow.* Harper & Row, 1985.

McCully, Emily Arnold. *Picnic.* HarperCollins, 1984.

Omerod, Jan. *Moonlight.* Lothrop, 1982.

Peek, Merle. *Roll Over! A Counting Book.* Clarion Books, 1981.

Turkle, Brinton. *Deep in the Forest.* E.P. Dutton, 1976.

Sing-along

Aliki. *Hush, Little Baby: A Folk Lullaby.* Simon & Schuster, 1968.

Carle, Eric. *Today Is Monday.* Scholastic, 1993.

Child, L.M. *Over the River and Through the Wood.* Little, Brown & Co., 1989.

Kozikowski, Renate. *The Teddy Bear's Picnic.* Macmillan, 1982.

Peek, Merle. *Mary Wore Her Red Dress, and Henry Wore His Green Sneakers.* Clarion, 1985.

Raffi. *Baby Beluga.* Crown, 1990.

Raffi. *One Light, One Sun.* Crown, 1988.

Raffi. *Wheels on the Bus.* Crown, 1988.

Seeger, Pete. *Abiyoyo.* Macmillan, 1986.

Spier, Peter. *The Fox Went Out on a Chilly Night.* Doubleday, 1961.

Zuromski, Diane. *The Farmer in the Dell.* Little, Brown & Co., 1978.

Classic Stories

Brown, Marcia. *Stone Soup.* Scribners, 1947.

Galdone, Paul. *The Three Billy Goats Gruff.* Clarion, 1973.

Galdone, Paul. **Henny Penny.** Clarion, 1968.

Galdone, Paul. **The Gingerbread Boy.** Clarion, 1975.

Galdone, Paul. **The Three Bears.** Clarion, 1973.

Galdone, Paul. **The Teeny Tiny Woman.** Clarion, 1984.

Potter, Beatrix. **The Tale of Peter Rabbit.** Warne, 1902.

Rey, H.A. **Curious George.** Houghton Mifflin, 1941.

Slobodkina, Esphyr. **Caps for Sale.** Harper & Row, 1940.

K-1 Stories

Allen, Pamela. **Who Sank the Boat?** Coward-McCann, 1982.

Coward, Wanda Gag. **Millions of Cats.** Putnam, 1928.

Flack, Marjorie. **Ask Mr. Bear.** Macmillan, 1932.

Hutchins, Pat. **Rosie's Walk.** Macmillan, 1968.

Keats, Ezra Jack. **The Snowy Day.** Scholastic, 1962.

McCloskey, Robert. **Make Way for Ducklings.** Scholastic, 1941.

Seuss, Dr. **One Fish, Two Fish, Red Fish, Blue Fish.** Beginner Books, 1960.

Tafuri, Nancy. **Have You Seen My Duckling?** Greenwillow, 1984.

Waddell, Martin. **Owl Babies.** Candlewick Press, 1992.

Animals

Carle, Eric. **The Mixed-Up Chameleon.** Thomas Y. Crowell, 1975.

Carle, Eric. **The Very Hungry Caterpillar.** Philomel, 1969.

Carle, Eric. **The Very Busy Spider.** Philomel, 1985.

Ehlert, Lois. **Feathers for Lunch.** Harcourt Brace Jovanovich, 1990.

Gibbons, Gail. **Spiders.** Holiday House, 1993.

Goldin, Augusta. **Ducks Don't Get Wet.** Thomas Y. Crowell, 1965.

Heller, Ruth. **Chickens Aren't the Only Ones.** Grosset and Dunlap, 1981.

Parker, Nancy W. and Joan R. Wright. **Bugs.** Greenwillow, 1987.

Patterson, Francine. *Koko's Kitten.* Scholastic, 1985.

Bears

Degen, Bruce. *Jamberry*. Harper & Row, 1983.

Freeman, Don. *Corduroy*. Viking, 1968.

Jonas, Ann. *Two Bear Cubs.* Greenwillow, 1982.

Ward, Lynd. *The Biggest Bear.* Houghton Mifflin, 1952.

Colors

Goennel, Heidi. *Colors.* Little, Brown & Co., 1990.

Heller, Ruth. *Color.* Putnam & Grossett, 1995.

Jonas, Ann. *Color Dance.* Greenwillow, 1989.

Kirkpatrick, Rena K. *Rainbow Colors.* Steck-Vaughn, 1991.

McMillan, Bruce. *Growing Colors.* Lothrop, Lee & Shepard, 1988.

Sawicki, Norma Jean. *The Little Red House.* Lothrop, Lee & Shepard, 1989.

Serfozo, Mary. *Who Said Red?* Margaret K. McElderry, 1989.

Walsh, Ellen Stoll. *Mouse Paint.* Harcourt Brace Jovanovich, 1989.

Westray, Kathleen. *A Color Sampler.* Ticknor & Fields, 1993.

Dinosaurs

Aliki. *Dinosaur Bones.* Thomas Y. Crowell, 1988.

Aliki. *Digging Up Dinosaurs.* Thomas Y. Crowell, 1981.

Barton, Byron. *Dinosaurs, Dinosaurs.* Thomas Y. Crowell, 1989.

Clark, Mary Lou. *Dinosaurs: A New True Book.* Childrens Press, 1981.

Pallotta, Jerry. *The Dinosaur Alphabet Book.* Charlesbridge, 1991.

Parish, Peggy. *Dinosaur Time.* Harper & Row, 1974.

Family

Bauer, Caroline Feller. ***My Mom Travels a Lot.*** Frederick Warne, 1981.

Bernhard, Emery. ***A Ride on Mother's Back: A Day of Baby Carrying Around the World.*** Harcourt Brace, 1996.

Flournoy, Valerie. ***The Patchwork Quilt.*** Dial, 1985.

Havill, Juanita. ***Jamaica Tag-Along.*** Houghton Mifflin, 1989.

Kraus, Robert. ***Whose Mouse Are You?*** Greenwillow, 1982.

Levinson, Riki. ***I Go with My Family to Grandma's.*** Puffin, 1986.

Long, Earlene. ***Gone Fishing.*** Houghton Mifflin, 1984.

Polacco, Patricia. ***My Rotten Redheaded Older Brother.*** Simon & Schuster, 1994.

Rotner, Shelley and Sheila M. Kelly. ***Lots of Moms.*** Dial, 1996.

Rylant, Cynthia. ***The Relatives Came.*** Bradbury, 1985.

Weiss, Nicki. ***Waiting.*** Greenwillow, 1981.

Farms

Azarian, Mary. ***A Farmer's Alphabet.*** D.R. Godine, 1981.

Brown, Margaret Wise. ***Big Red Barn.*** Harper & Row, 1989.

Daniel, Alan. ***Old MacDonald Had a Farm.*** The Wright Group, 1992.

Rae, Mary Maki. ***The Farmer in the Dell.*** Viking Penguin, 1988.

Tafuri, Nancy. ***Early Morning in the Barn.*** Greenwillow, 1983.

Friendship

Aliki. ***We Are Best Friends.*** Greenwillow, 1982.

Hale, Sarah Josepha. ***Mary Had a Little Lamb.*** Holiday House, 1984.

Hallinan, P.K. ***That's What a Friend Is.*** Childrens Press, 1977.

Hoban, Russell. ***Best Friends for Frances.*** HarperCollins, 1969.

Hutchins, Pat. ***My Best Friend.*** Greenwillow, 1993.

Hutchins, Pat. **Titch and Daisy.** Greenwillow, 1996.

Leedy, Loreen. **How Humans Make Friends.** Holiday House, 1996.

Math

Bang, Molly. **Ten, Nine, Eight.** Greenwillow, 1983.

Crews, Donald. **Ten Black Dots.** Greenwillow, 1986.

Ehlert, Lois. **Fish Eyes.** Harcourt Brace Jovanovich, 1990.

Garne, S.T. **One White Sail: A Caribbean Counting Book.** Simon & Schuster, 1992.

MacCarthy, Patricia. **Ocean Parade: A Counting Book.** Dial, 1990.

McMillan, Bruce. **Eating Fractions.** Scholastic, 1992.

McMillan, Bruce. **Jelly Beans for Sale.** Scholastic, 1996.

McMillan, Bruce. **One, Two, One Pair!** Scholastic, 1991.

Noll, Sally. **Off and Counting.** Greenwillow, 1984.

Rees, Mary. **Ten in a Bed.** Little, Brown & Co., 1988.

Sloat, Terri. **From One to One Hundred.** Dutton, 1991.

Schwartz, David M. **How Much Is a Million?** Lothrop, 1985.

Nature

Cherry, Lynne. **The Great Kapok Tree: A Tale of the Amazon Rain Forest.** Harcourt Brace Jovanovich, 1990.

Ehlert, Lois. **Planting a Rainbow.** Harcourt Brace Jovanovich, 1988.

Ehlert, Lois. **Growing Vegetable Soup.** Harcourt Brace Jovanovich, 1987.

Guiberson, Brenda Z. **Cactus Hotel.** Henry Holt, 1991.

Krauss, Ruth. **The Carrot Seed.** Harper & Row, 1945.

Lyon, George. **ABCEDAR.** Franklin Watts, 1989.

Micucci, Charles. **The Life and Times of the Apple.** Orchard Books, 1992.

Seasons

Ehlert, Lois. **Red Leaf, Yellow Leaf.** Harcourt Brace Jovanovich, 1991.

Ets, Marie Hall. **Gilberto and the Wind.** Viking, 1963.

Krauss, Ruth. **The Happy Day.** Harper & Row, 1949.

Rockwell, Anne and Harlow Rockwell. **The First Snowfall.** Macmillan, 1987.

Morgan, Allen. **Sadie and the Snowman.** Scholastic, 1985.

Neitzel, Shirley. **The Jacket I Wear in the Snow.** Greenwillow, 1989.

Teacher Resources

Lipson, Eden Ross. **Parent's Guide to the Best Books for Students.** Times Books, 1988.

Piña, Jeanne and Katherine Maitland. **Poetry Power ESL.** Modern Curriculum Press, 1993.

Raines, Shirley C. and Robert J. Canady. **Story S-T-R-E-T-C-H-E-R-S: Activities to Expand Children's Favorite Books.** Gryphon House, 1989.

Routman, Regie. **Invitations.** Heinemann, 1991.

Smallwood, Betty Ansin. **The Literature Connection: A Read-Aloud Guide for Multicultural Classrooms.** Addison-Wesley, 1991.

Thiessen, Diane and Margaret Matthias (eds.). **The Wonderful World of Mathematics: A Critically Annotated List of Children's Books in Mathematics.** The National Council of Teachers of Mathematics, 1992.

Welchman-Tischler, Rosamond. **How to Use Children's Literature to Teach Mathematics.** The National Council of Teachers of Mathematics, 1992.

Chapter 3

Listening and Speaking

Listening, speaking, reading, and writing work together to reinforce language and learning. If these skill areas are integrated throughout the day, English-language learners can use them to make meaningful connections. Although the divisions are somewhat artificial, listening and speaking will be discussed in this section, and reading and writing in subsequent sections.

Real progress in learning a language requires that we build on students' listening skills. English learners need lots of "comprehensible input," that is, language that conveys a message. What they hear should not be too much beyond their language level, but it should stretch and engage them in trying to develop meaning.

As they acquire English, students experience varying levels in their ability to respond. First they go through a stage of attending to the language. They tend to answer nonverbally or give yes or no responses. In fact, many cross-cultural students experience a silent period before they begin to speak (Dulay, 1982). This period may last from a few days to several months. Do not try to force students to speak during this time. They are adjusting to their new environment and absorbing language in a normal way.

After this prespeaking period, students move to an "early production" phase, giving one-word answers or short phrases (Krashen & Terrell, 1983). Gradually, speech emerges, and students use longer chunks of language. As they continue to interact, their output more closely approximates standard English.

It takes great energy and concentration to listen to a new language for long periods. Most of your beginning ESL students will tire, tune out, or daydream. Give them breaks during the day to regroup and refresh themselves.

One method of teaching language, Total Physical Response (TPR), emphasizes listening (Asher, 1988). It is used in many ESL and foreign-language classes. The teacher gives commands and acts them out, while students perform the same actions with her. Through these demonstrations, commands such as "Open the door" and "Put the pencil on the table" become immediately understandable. Because comprehension is reinforced through activity and there is no pressure to speak, anxiety is low.

Gradually, students can perform the actions without teacher modeling. As students progress, the teacher increases the complexity of the language, still using commands. Students begin to speak when they are ready. At that point, they act as the teacher, giving commands for others to follow.

TPR is especially helpful in the initial stages of language learning because it provides students with a large amount of language they can understand immediately. Work with students, using simple commands and physical responses. As they become confident, move to more complex commands.

Introductory Activities

Fold listening and speaking activities into your daily program. These activities need to be uncontrived and purposeful. A good way to achieve this is to make them a part of your theme studies. Give students lots of opportunities to work at their level. Although students at early stages may not speak very much, they are still capable of understanding content. Organize the activities into the following four stages, and adapt them to the level of your students.

1. **Preparation** Tap students' background knowledge and set the purpose for the activity.

2. **Listening Task** Provide a listening task through speaking, reading stories aloud, telling stories, and using audiotapes, videos, and CD-ROM materials.

3. **Student Response** Give students an opportunity to respond.

4. **Debrief** Review their responses with them: What made this an easy or difficult activity? What can they try next time?

Listening and Nonverbal Responses

Adapt the following suggestions to the language levels of your students. These activities also serve as opportunities for you to observe students and assess their comprehension. The suggestions marked 𝔅 are especially suited for beginners.

𝔅 **Follow Directions** Start with one-step directions. As students' language proficiency increases, give directions with two or more steps.

Give students commands they can respond to with physical movements. Examples: *Stand next to Kwong. Clap your hands slowly/loudly/with excitement. Go to the chalkboard and underline the first word in the sentence.*

Have students follow directions to make or build things. For instance, students can engage in paper-folding and paper-cutting activities; building with plastic or wooden blocks; or creating step-by-step art, such as prints or models.

Give directions for students to mark pictures, maps, or charts.

𝔅 **Point to the Answer** When working with visuals such as posters, transparencies, or pictures, ask students questions and let them point. This way, you supply the oral language, and they demonstrate comprehension. Reinforce their responses after they point to the pictures by rephrasing or expanding the language.

𝔅 **Response Cards** Distribute index cards with happy faces and sad faces, numerals, math symbols, or words. When you ask a question, students respond with the appropriate cue card. Use this technique when you want to involve all students in a quick comprehension check. For example, read a short story to students, then follow up with questions that students can answer with yes or no. This also works well for nonfiction material, much like a true-or-false quiz.

𝔅 **Pantomime** Invite students to pantomime a story as you read it aloud a second or third time.

𝔅 **Bingo** This game can be modified for many levels. Remember to use it within a context, not as a "drill" exercise. Copy and distribute the

"Bingo Grid" reproducible on page 92. On the bingo grid, you can incorporate pictures of vocabulary items from science, social studies, or language arts; pictures of actions, events, or characters from a story; or answer choices to math problems.

B Voting Invite students to show preferences by voting. Let students select a favorite story by signing their names on the appropriate chart. Or make a graph and have students write their names on sticky notes and place them in the appropriate column. You might also divide the classroom into regions and have students group themselves according to their choice.

Which story did you like better? Vote for your favorite story.

The Very Hungry Caterpillar	The Very Busy Spider
Ramon	Yuki
Becky	Nora
Takeesha	
Ahmed	

Ⓑ Sequencing/Choosing Pictures Display pictures and ask students to sequence them as you read a short story or text. Or provide two or more similar pictures and have students choose the one you describe.

Ⓑ Art Ask students to respond to the listening event by drawing a picture. To guide students, ask questions such as, "What do you think the main character looked like?" Show why the setting was so scary. Show what happened at the end of the story.

Listening and Spoken/Written Responses

Adapt the following suggestions to the language levels of your students. These activities also serve as opportunities for you to observe students and assess their comprehension. The first suggestion, marked Ⓑ is especially suited for beginners. The next three are progressively challenging.

Ⓑ Brief Verbal Responses After listening to a short story or watching a video, ask students questions that require yes-or-no, true-or-false, or other one-word answers. Examples: *What is this animal? What do giraffes eat? Do giraffes have short necks? Do giraffes live in Brazil or in Africa?*

Depending on the English proficiency of students, you can ask questions requiring short answers. Examples: *How long did it take for the cookies to bake? What ingredients did we use? How is the dough different from the baked cookie?*

Brief Written Responses Ask students to write their responses to questions such as the ones listed previously in the Brief Verbal Responses section.

Note-taking Have students use note-taking skills. Show them how to listen for and jot down key words, information, or data. Give them graphic organizers to provide cues for listening. Use simple outlines that have some parts missing. Ask students to fill in the information as they listen. After the activity, have them compare and discuss their notes with a partner.

Journal Entries Ask students to write personal and reflective responses in their journals. You may wish to model writing a journal entry and provide help as needed.

THINGS TO REMEMBER

- Listening is an active, dynamic activity.

- Listening requires great concentration and energy.

- Listeners need a chance to respond to the input.

- Language learners need frequent breaks from listening.

Speaking Activities

Adapt the following suggestions to the language levels of your students. These activities also serve as opportunities for you to observe students and assess their comprehension. The suggestions marked 𝕭 are especially suited for beginners.

Games The list of games is almost endless. The following chart describes games you can adapt to many situations and language levels. For instance, the guessing game can be adapted to almost any content area, including social studies, science, or language arts.

𝕭 I'm the Teacher	Let volunteers take the part of the teacher to give students commands to act out, to call out bingo cards, or to give directions to the group.
Brainstorming Lists	Students work in teams to think of items related to a given topic. Or let them use reference materials, such as posters and picture dictionaries, to add to their list. You may also have them generate questions about a topic.
Guessing	Let a volunteer choose a picture from a set. The rest of the group takes turns asking questions to try to guess what the picture is. Or tape a picture on the back of a volunteer. He must ask questions of the group to see if he can determine what the picture is.

𝕭 Songs, Chants, and Poetry Music and poetry provide chunks of powerful language. Singing and chanting help students with the natural sound of language. Many song books and picture books have excellent illustrations that support the words and provide context. (See the Read-Aloud book list section on pages 32–39.)

𝕭 Sentence Patterns This does not need to be a drill or copy exercise if you use it within context and if students are asked to make personal responses. Provide a model of an open sentence and allow students to complete it.

Feelings	I'm happy when _____. I'm sad when _____.
Likes/Dislikes	I like _____, but I don't like_____. My family likes to _____.
Preferences	I like _____ the best. My favorite _____ is _____.
Wants/Desires/ Wishes	For my birthday, I want_____. When I grow up I want to be _____. Someday, I would like to_____.

Oral Storytelling Demonstrations and modeling help students get a feel for this type of activity. Students can tell their stories orally to individuals or small groups. Guide students in preparing for their storytelling. Have them use storyboards, story maps, pictures, clay models, or other props. You might copy and distribute the "Tell a Story" reproducible on page 93. Model how to complete it. Have students tape a story so you can listen to it. Then tape a response back so they can listen to you.

Discussions Help students acquire discussion skills. Model and talk about such skills as active listening, turn-taking, keeping the discussion going, asking questions, and drawing conclusions.

Putting It All Together: Interviews

Interviews give ESL students opportunities to interact socially and use language for authentic purposes. It takes several strategies to conduct interviews successfully: getting an interviewee's attention; speaking clearly; repeating information; asking for clarification; and asking follow-up questions.

Even beginning English-language learners can participate in interviews, if you modify the task to their level. They can use yes or no questions that start with the words "Do you like. . . ?" to conduct surveys. They can also ask "or" questions, such as, "Which do you like, pizza or hamburgers?" and other forced-choice questions. Using these more limited questions will give them control in understanding responses.

Classroom Profile

To help students get started with interviewing, do a Classroom Profile with them at the beginning of the school year. Adjust the types of questions to their language levels.

1. **Preparation** Explain to students that they will be conducting short interviews to find out about every person in the class. Discuss what kinds of information they would like to know about their classmates. Give them some examples, such as, What is your favorite TV show? How many languages do you speak? List students' ideas on a chart and post it in the room.

   Copy and distribute one of the three "Survey" reproducibles on pages 94–96. Review the directions. Or show students how to construct an interview form by writing the question at the top and preparing a place to record the data or responses.

2. **Rehearsal** Model how to conduct an interview. Ask for volunteers and role-play the situation, demonstrating how to record the responses. Have pairs of students select a question and rehearse their interview. Work with English-language learners on stress and intonation patterns used in asking questions. Model the language by asking the questions naturally. Point out how one's voice goes up and down.

3. **Conduct the Interview** Throughout the day, give students time to conduct their interviews.

4. **Follow-up Activities** After the interviews, demonstrate how to use the information gathered. Show the class how to make bar graphs or pie charts. Lead the class in drawing conclusions. Model the language: *Five students like hamburgers. Eight students like tacos. Twelve students like pizza the best. Pizza is Room 15's favorite fast food.*

Let students work with partners to show their interview responses in a visual format, such as graphs and illustrated posters. Ask them to write a summary statement. Display their work on a bulletin board titled "A Profile of Our Room," or "A Picture of Our Class."

CONDUCTING AN INTERVIEW ACTIVITY

1. **Preparation** Set the stage. Decide what information is needed and why.

2. **Rehearsal** Role-play the interview. Work on intonation and stress patterns. Practice recording the responses.

3. **Conducting the Interview** This is the real-life situation!

4. **Follow-up Activities** Compile data, construct graphs or charts, make summary statements, or write reports.

Once students feel comfortable interviewing, you can help them choose among the following activities, according to their language level.

INTERVIEW ACTIVITIES
Mini-Interviews

- Partner work: Ask simple, prepared questions.

- Polls with a yes-or-no answer: "Do you like to swim?"

- Surveys with a forced-choice question: "Which class do you like best: art, gym, or music?"

- Surveys with a one-word answer (open-ended): "What is your favorite sport?"

Extended Interviews

- Get to know people: Ask questions to become acquainted.

- Gather information about people or events: Find out about a school fair, bake sale, field trip, guest speakers.

- Interview classmates about special hobbies, trips, projects, and accomplishments.

———————————

Chapter 4

Reading

Tackeyong is a five-year-old kindergarten student who arrived in the U.S. from South Korea less than one year ago. He spent several months in what the teacher described as a "sour mood." At times he was uncooperative and belligerent.

In the spring, Tackeyong appeared happier and began playing with the other students. His spoken language, although very limited, began to emerge. His parents reported that he was reading Korean at home. In a short time, he was reading print around the school and simple picture books in English. (His bilingual tutor reported that Tackeyong could retell the stories in Korean.) Tackeyong's understanding of English and ability in reading seemed to exceed his verbal skills.

Lin is a fourth grader from China who has been in the U.S. for two and a half years. When she reads aloud, she makes many errors. Yet Lin demonstrates understanding of the material when she answers questions and participates in class discussions.

Can students who do not have control over English take part in literacy events? Yes! As the experiences of Tackeyong and Lin show, second-language learners can make sense of print. Reading will stimulate and reinforce their learning. Taking part in purposeful academic activities gives them confidence that they are growing as English-language learners. Students on all levels of the language learning continuum need opportunities for developing literacy.

In the complex process of reading, ESL students use the context of the reading situation, their life experiences, knowledge of the language, and the written word to build meaning. As students interact with the text, they make predictions, eliminating or accepting them as they read.

Material within students' cultural, cognitive, and experiential range allows them to make meaning from print. It is easy to understand this point if you think of the times you have tried to read material beyond your experience—perhaps a car insurance policy or a computer manual. Comprehension lowers dramatically when negotiating unfamiliar territory. It is no different for second-language learners. If students are inexperienced with the cultural, social, or informational context, comprehension is undermined.

Hima is a second grader who came from India nearly three years ago. She enjoys reading and choosing library books to read. Recently, she experienced great difficulty with a theme on fairy tales. The teacher couldn't pinpoint the source of the trouble until she realized that Hima had never heard "Little Red Riding Hood" or other Western stories.

When second-language learners read, they look through cultural glasses. Students' personal backgrounds will influence what they get from the printed word. To "add English" they will need to experience and understand aspects of the new culture.

Hima's teacher assumed all students had prior knowledge of a variety of fairy tales. But Hima needed to hear, read, and experience traditional Western stories to participate in such activities as comparing and contrasting fairy tales. Hima's teacher also could have helped Hima make connections by using tales from India or other stories that Hima and her family could share.

Daniel arrived from Israel a few months ago. He has thrown himself into the life of his first-grade classroom with gusto. His oral skills have blossomed. When he reads from his first-grade book, he appears to be a fluid reader. Daniel and his teacher are puzzled. Although he can say the words, he does not always understand what they mean.

Daniel became an expert at sounding out words, as his teacher had taught him. Yet knowing how to say the words did not help him with their meanings. Daniel needed other strategies to comprehend what he was reading. Telling students like Daniel to slow down and sound out unfamiliar words will not make them better readers. These students need to develop strategies to build their vocabulary in English, such as finding context clues, skipping unknown words, and using background knowledge.

Tapping Students' Prior Knowledge

Tapping prior knowledge can help you assess students' levels of experience and personal knowledge of the topic. What are their attitudes and perceptions about this topic? Is it potentially relevant to students? What misconceptions do they have? Do they lack awareness about important cultural points? How do their experiences relate to the topic? You will also learn what language and vocabulary they understand and can use. What language structures might help them be more articulate?

The following methods can help you assess students' prior knowledge.

- Ask a bilingual tutor to work with students in their home languages. Students can reveal their knowledge and experiences. Using the first language is particularly important when students have very limited control of English.

- Ask students to talk about the topic and tell you what they know. Jotting down their comments in a class log will allow you to reuse this information later, to clear up misconceptions, or to expand on what is being learned.

- Think about several subtopics for your theme and use word associations (Holmes & Roser, 1987). Give students a word related to your subtopic and ask them to tell what they know about it. Word association may be especially helpful in assessing students' vocabulary.

- Structured questions require more preparation. After dividing your theme into subtopics, list several questions for each. Use the questions to discover what students do and don't know. The information will guide you in selecting materials and designing lessons to extend their knowledge.

Once you have an idea of students' prior knowledge, you can plan for activities that will build on it. You can also design activities that will help students become aware of important cultural information. Use whatever materials you have, such as filmstrips, videos, computers, pictures, posters, magazines, charts, picture books, books on tape, and student-written books.

Adapt the materials for the language level of students. You might turn off the sound on a video and provide a narration that uses simpler language. Pause often to check for comprehension. Rerun sections of the video that seem helpful.

Building Vocabulary

One of the obvious differences between ESL students and native speakers is that students who are acquiring English are learning basic vocabulary while they are also trying to function academically. Often, you will be surprised at their gaps in word knowledge. Other times they will astound you with how much they have acquired in a short time. In any case, vocabulary building is a top priority for ESL students.

How students learn new words depends on their learning styles, strategies, motivation, and needs. Some students will make long lists and keep them handy to study and use. Others will refuse any controlled approach and will seem to wing it.

Most beginners sense a need for certain language functions, such as asking for help, and adopt the vocabulary. They quickly learn words that are important to them, such as *lunchroom, bathroom, recess,* and *playground.* The key for learning vocabulary is the need—the immediate relevance to students' lives. It is more difficult to maintain this level of need when you approach certain academic tasks. Tapping into students' curiosity and love for learning will motivate them to learn academics.

Many years ago, Sylvia Ashton-Warner (1963) developed a method of teaching Maori kindergartners how to read. She gave them cards on which she printed *key vocabulary:* words students chose for themselves. These words had intense personal meanings and connections to students' lives, and they were used for a variety of literacy activities. Even older students can collect personal words that they find interesting, unusual, and useful. In a short time they will compile a large word-bank.

Meaningful use of vocabulary is perhaps the best way to ensure that students learn new words. Ask yourself: Can they use language for real purposes—to explain, predict, describe, complain, and persuade?

Activities to Help Students Develop Vocabulary

The words you speak to define an unfamiliar word will "evaporate" within minutes, leaving behind little trace of its meaning. Learning vocabulary is not a passive process. Students must interact with language and use it purposefully.

Use or adapt the following suggestions to help students extend their vocabulary.

- Read aloud picture books, stories, and magazine articles. Discuss the meaning of powerful and rich language. Use your voice, gestures, and drama to emphasize meaning.

- Themes are perhaps the best way to create a context; to introduce and use vocabulary in meaningful ways; and to recycle language by integrating a topic into several content areas.

- Some proponents of whole language may argue that role-playing may be too artificial—the situation is not real and lacks authenticity. ESL students, however, are motivated when they realize that the language is something they need and can make their own. If students can see the relevance to their immediate needs, such as role-playing how to ask for information, they will delight in acting out situations.

- Have classmates pantomime the meanings of words and phrases.

- Use a combination of quick sketches, real objects, and role-plays to demonstrate the meaning of the word.

- Use familiar synonyms and antonyms.

- Categorize new vocabulary items by placing them within familiar conceptual groups, such as Farm Animals, Parts of the Body, or Character Traits.

- Help students put new items, or pictures of items, on a scale or a chart of familiar words.

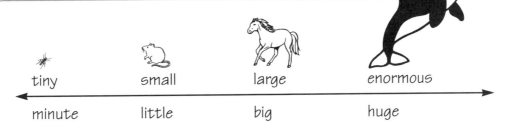

tiny	small	large	enormous
minute	little	big	huge

- Have students make illustrated word-banks to use as reference tools for class work. These may be individual or class-sized posters and charts.

- When studying a particular topic, invite students to work in collaborative groups to make ABC books or picture dictionaries.

- Ask students to help you label classroom displays with words, phrases, or sentences.

- Ask older students to relate new vocabulary items to their home language or culture. For example, to most of us in the U.S. the word *family* means immediate members, such as a mother, father, sister, and brother. Perhaps to an ESL student the word *family* also encompasses uncles, aunts, cousins, or grandparents who may live with them.

What comes to mind when you hear the word *bread*? Is it a long baguette? A slice of whole-wheat toast? A corn tortilla? A pocket bread? Familiar words like *bread*, *family*, or *home* may appear to have simple meanings. Yet because these concepts are embedded in culture, people picture them in different ways. Learning English involves becoming aware of American culture and the meaning it gives the language.

"WHAT PEOPLE THINK OF WHEN THEY HEAR THE WORD BREAD . . ."

Brazilians:
French bread

Americans:
toast

Mexicans:
tortillas

Syrians:
pocket bread

Five-Minute Vocabulary Games for Beginners

Play quick and easy games with less experienced English-language learners to help them internalize vocabulary. As always, remember that these games should unfold from established contexts, such as content area studies and theme cycles.

Surprise Box Prepare a surprise box, placing several objects inside. A volunteer reaches in without looking, feels the object, and tries to guess what it is. For a more challenging activity, have a student select an object, then call on volunteers to ask questions about it, such as, "Is it smooth?" or "Is it green?" After several questions, the class should try to guess the item.

I'm Thinking of . . . Display pictures or objects. Select one without identifying your choice and provide clues. Call on volunteers to guess what it is. Example: I'm thinking of an animal. It is very large. It lives on land. It has a trunk. *(an elephant)* When students are familiar with this game, let volunteers take turns giving clues.

Picture Time Display a set of pictures on one theme or topic. Invite students to sort the pictures into categories. Invite more experienced students to tell why or how they grouped the pictures.

Display a set of pictures that shows more than three pairs of opposites. Have students pair the words that correspond to the pictures. As an alternative, invite volunteers to choose and identify a picture. They, in turn, choose classmates to pantomime the opposite. More experienced students may tell about the pictures. Example: *I get hot in the summer. But I'm cold when it snows.* They may also write the word pairs.

Display two sets, one of pictures and another with words, phrases, or sentences on cards. Ask students to match the word cards with the pictures. As a follow-up, have students make their own sentences for the pictures.

Prepare word cards from word banks that students have accumulated during your theme study. A student from one team draws a word card from the set and reads it to the class. A member of another team must pantomime the word. As an alternate activity, play charades. Have one team draw a word card, read it silently, then pantomime its meaning. Members from the opposing team must guess the word.

Bingo This is a favorite game because it involves all students at the same time and because it can be so easily adapted to different ability levels. Each child will need a bingo grid and markers. Copy and distribute the "Bingo Grid" on page 92 or create your own. From a predetermined set, students draw pictures or paste small copies of pictures in each square.

For word bingo, have students choose words and write them on the grid. The leader must have a master set of cards for all the pictures or all the words. Using this master set, the leader draws a card and identifies it for the group. Students place markers on their grids as the cards are identified.

Putting It All Together: The Language Experience Approach

The language experience approach (LEA) has been used for many years with preschool and kindergarten students to help them develop literacy. The LEA can also help English learners develop oral skills and make connections between speaking and the printed word.

The first step in the LEA is a shared activity that engages students and is meaningful to them. A cooking activity, a walk around the neighborhood, and a simple science experiment are examples of shared activities. Prepare for the activity by thinking about the desired learning outcomes, key words, and language needed. You may also want to think about how this activity connects with other experiences students have had.

Suppose your class has been studying grains and breads from around the world. You want your class to work in small groups to make corn bread. In some cases, one group could demonstrate the activity while others watch.

1. Find a simple recipe for corn bread. Make a large rebus poster that shows the steps for making corn bread. Prepare students for the activity. Introduce the ingredients and match them with the words on the recipe chart.

INGREDIENTS LIST FOR CORN BREAD

2. As students make the corn bread, encourage as much language use as possible. If students are quietly observing, you may make the language explicit. If they gesture, you can provide the spoken equivalent. If they use single words or short phrases, you can extend their language by rephrasing.

Teacher: What do you do next?

Rosa: Milk!

Teacher: Yes. We add the milk. Pour 1/2 cup of milk into the bowl. What is Rosa doing now, class?

Students: Mixing.

Teacher: Right. She's mixing everything. She's stirring. Look, the cornmeal is getting wet. See?

3. While the corn bread is baking, gather students around you. Talk about what happened during the activity. Help students retell the sequence of events. Use props or a list of key words to help students formulate their ideas. If necessary, expand on what students say.

4. Immediately after the review, have the group dictate a story about making corn bread. As they tell you the story, write it in clear print on a large chart.

5. After a complete story is written, read it to the class, sweeping your hand across the page as you read. Then ask the entire group to read it with you, perhaps several times. Again, follow the words by pointing. Invite two or three students to do a choral reading. Finally, ask volunteers to read the story for the group.

6. Lead students in a series of follow-up activities. Have volunteers circle content words, such as *cornmeal* or *milk*. Ask them to see how many times they can find these words in the story. Point to the word *mix* or *pour* and ask students to pantomime its meaning.

Copy the story onto sentence strips. Ask volunteers to match the strips to the printed story. Ask the class to sequence the sentence strips in the appropriate order or to retell the whole story. Invite them to choose a sentence strip and illustrate it.

The language experience approach can be adapted to a variety of language levels and ages. Some students may want to copy the LEA stories to take home and read to their parents. Others can select words from the story and add them to their word banks. More experienced students may be asked to write their own stories and share them with partners. You can also make the LEA activities more cognitively demanding by planning challenging activities such as science experiments.

While using the language experience approach, remember to make language explicit and to use the shared activity as a base for a variety of extension and follow-up activities that recycle and expand students' language.

Chapter 5

Writing

Have you ever composed a letter or written a story in another language? If so, you probably felt uneasy, constrained by your lack of control of the language. That is how ESL students feel when they try to write. They sense that expressing themselves in English makes them sound "dumb" or babyish. When such negative emotions are stirred up, it is easy for students to give in to frustration.

If we pay attention to *what* students are trying to say instead of *how* they say it, students will take more risks in writing. Their grammar and writing conventions will eventually look more like standard English. This process requires time, patience, and a belief that growth will take place.

Time is a gift we give our students—time to think, time to make connections, and time to create. Soon, English learners will perceive the power unleashed through writing. Through the process they will find the voice in which to communicate their messages and to tell their stories.

As with listening, speaking, and reading, writing unfolds when classroom interactions focus on meaning. The skills of writing can be taught within the framework of communicative activities.

Supporting Students' Writing

Students need to use language for real purposes: to express, to describe, to inform, to complain, and to show appreciation. Link classroom activities with these missions. For example, ask students to write about their positive or negative experiences, such as interesting new discoveries or problems with other students. Have them vote their preferences or choices by writing them on slips of paper to be collected and tallied.

Combine writing with attendance, calendar activities, daily news, class schedules, and other routine classroom procedures. ESL students often need help in understanding special events and holidays. Copy and distribute the "Calendar Grid" reproducible on page 97. Provide a calendar to use as a model, then have students make personal calendars on which to record important events and dates. Young students can mark holidays with stickers.

The writing process gives English-language learners a predictable pattern for their work—a framework that supports their efforts. Make sure students think about their intended audience, whether that audience is comprised of partners, classmates, other school students, their family, a teacher, or the principal. They will develop a sense that language changes according to the audience and the reason for writing. You might copy and distribute the "Writing Plan" reproducible on page 98. Use writing examples and persons in the classroom to illustrate some of the answer choices, such as *book* or *teacher*.

Support the writing efforts of your second-language learners in the following ways.

Build Context Use concrete experiences and activities as springboards to writing. Integrate classroom instruction in theme cycles so that concepts and language are recycled and refined. Extend what is happening in the classroom. For example, have the class write letters of invitation for an open house. Or have them write letters to thank guest speakers. Copy and distribute the "Letter Form" reproducible on page 99. Model how to write a friendly letter, using the form.

Visual Support Give students visual support by brainstorming lists of key words and phrases. Post illustrated lists of important words as aids. Display labeled charts, pictures, and posters as references for writing activities. Encourage drawings, sketches, and other artwork as part of the writing process.

Reading Reading aloud will help students internalize the rhythm of language. Read a variety of genres for a variety of purposes. Discuss authors' intentions and how the information is conveyed.

Writing Samples Provide several samples of a specific writing activity. Study at least one example carefully with students to help them internalize language and think about how a piece might look, read, and sound.

Model the Writing Talk through the writing task, demonstrating for students the types of thinking involved. Use an overhead projector or large sheets of newsprint to list the steps in the writing task. Point out writing conventions and useful linguistic markers, such as *once upon a time, first,* and *finally.*

Supported Practice Provide supported practice until students can function independently. Compose group stories, letters, and messages. Write as students dictate. Keep these as examples for review. Have students use writing guides to give them direction as they think, talk, and write about their topic. These might include questions to answer, clustering, or graphic organizers. (Chapter 6 describes useful graphic organizers, with accompanying reproducibles.)

Guide small groups of students through the writing activity. For example, ask questions to clarify their message or provide suggestions for phrasing what they mean. Give feedback so they can make revisions.

Rehearse Before Writing Invite students to rehearse what they want to write about. Have them meet with partners to discuss their writing activity. Encourage listeners to ask their partners questions. Exchange partners and have them rehearse again.

BEGINNING ENGLISH-LANGUAGE LEARNERS CAN...

- Dictate words, sentences, or stories, then copy them.

- Copy environmental print, such as words to favorite songs, poems, or chants.

- Use drawing, sketching, and painting as springboards for writing.

- Complete open-ended sentences.

- Use poems, chants, songs, or predictable picture books as patterns for their writing.

- Sequence words or sentences to create a message or to summarize a story.

WRITING ACTIVITIES

- **Functional**

  writing name, age,
    address, phone number
    messages
  completing forms for
    tests or special requests
    annotated calendars

- **Personal**

  personal narratives
    letters (pen pal)
  postcards
  journal entries
    birthday, get-well cards
  thank-you notes

- **Academic**

  labels and captions
  songs, chants, riddles,
    jokes
  explaining solutions to
    problems
  keeping a learning log
  interviewing
  research notes
  informational reports
    book reports
  answering questions
  stories, plays, skits
    poems
  news reports, articles

Putting It All Together: Dialogue Journals

Dialogue journals are written conversations between you and the student that can last a few weeks or months (Kreeft, 1984). Dialogue journals provide students with authentic purposes for writing and serve as a bridge from talking to longer chunks of written discourse.

One drawback to using dialogue journals is the time needed to read, reflect, and respond to students. Some teachers respond to five or six journals per day, or cycle their journal writing in some predictable way so students can depend on the continuing dialogue.

In the first entry, tell about yourself, then ask one or two related open-ended questions for the student to respond to. This first entry may be copied and stapled into all students' notebooks.

Focus on the intended message, rather than on correcting mistakes. Incorporate the student's language, expanding and extending it in your response. Follow the student's topics, reacting genuinely to her interests, and you will notice how engaged you both will become!

Writing About Friends

Many writing tasks can be folded into themes or topic explorations. The ideas that follow support talking and writing about friends, a subject of special concern to ESL students.

Although the following suggestions are structured, you will also want to encourage students to write for a variety of purposes: free writing in journals, writing personal narratives about friends, creating stories, and recording information in learning logs.

Let students' interests and responses guide you in your selection of activities. Adjust the language to suit the level of your students.

Build Context/Reading Invite students to talk about pictures of friends playing together, sharing toys, and helping each other. *How Humans Make Friends* by Loreen Leedy (Holiday House, 1996) is a good book to read to the class. In this book an alien tells what he has observed about humans making friends. Two-page spreads with such headings as "How Friends Meet" and "Things Friends Do" are excellent discussion-starters.

Encourage students to work in teams to act out situations that show what it means to be a good friend. Use sections such as "Apologizing and Forgiving" from *How Humans Make Friends* to role-play those situations.

NEWCOMERS **may wish to work with bilingual parent volunteers to write letters or postcards to friends back home.**

Visual Support Have the class design posters titled "Ways to Greet Friends" and "Saying Goodbye to Friends." Invite cross-cultural students to share about their language and customs.

SAYING GOODBYE

- In English, the word *goodbye* is a shortened modern form of the phrase "*God be with you.*"

- Both the Portuguese word *adeus* and the Spanish word *adiós* mean "to God."

- The phrase *see you again* is the equivalent of the French *au revoir*, of the Chinese *ts'ai chien*, of the Spanish *hasta la vista*, and of the German *auf Wiedersehen*.

- The Japanese word *sayonara* means "if it must be so."

- The Hawaiian word *aloha* means "love."

- *Shalom*, a Hebrew greeting and farewell, means "peace."

(Berlitz, 1982)

Focus on Language Choose one aspect of language, such as descriptive words, to introduce to the class. Display pictures of various students for the class to describe. Provide a word bank and cards with phrases for less experienced students to match to corresponding pictures.

If students want to describe a friend, what kinds of information would they give? Together, make a web of categories, listing how the friend looks, what the friend likes to do, and so on.

Explore the meanings of more abstract concepts, such as words that describe character traits. Have students act out situations that exemplify the meanings, then have them match phrases with corresponding words. In the chart that follows, answers are shown in parentheses.

funny	helpful	friendly	kind	quiet

FRIENDLY OR NOT FRIENDLY?

talks to new kids at school	(friendly)
helps brother with homework	(helpful)
makes people laugh	(funny)
does nice things for others	(kind or helpful)
doesn't talk very much	(quiet)

Write the following statements on chart paper and read them aloud. Clarify any unfamiliar words. Have students work with partners to decide whether the person's action is friendly or unfriendly.

FRIENDLY OR NOT FRIENDLY?

- Roberto sat with the new boy during lunch.

- Daniel laughed when Manuel made a mistake in class.

- Linda dropped a box of crayons. Sandra helped her pick up the crayons.

This activity can be made more challenging by asking students to create their own statements. They can exchange papers with other groups to evaluate the statements.

Writing Samples Provide samples of the writing activity, such as the one in the following paragraph. These may be samples you have kept or ones you have written. Read the sample several times. Discuss the content as well as the mechanics.

My Friend Tony

I have a new friend. His name is Tony. He is nine years old. He has brown hair and brown eyes, just like me. In school, Tony enjoys math, science, and gym. He doesn't like spelling. Tony is a good soccer player, but his favorite sport is baseball. At home, he loves to play computer games.

Have less experienced students use the story in a controlled activity. You might suggest that they find and list all the descriptive words. Or you can scramble the sentences and let students work with partners to put them in order. Or you can scramble words within a sentence and have them write the sentence so it makes sense. Answers are shown in parentheses.

a. new a I friend have. (I have a new friend.)

b. name is His Tony. (His name is Tony.)

c. doesn't He spelling like. (He doesn't like spelling.)

Supported Practice Ask students to interview partners to learn more about them. Some students will be able to write their own questions. Less experienced students may use charts that you provide, such as the one that follows.

DO YOU LIKE TO . . .?

		YES	NO
	read books		
	play the piano		
	roller-skate		
	go shopping		
	play video games		
	other		

Model the Writing Demonstrate how you might write a paragraph describing a friend. Display a chart such as the one that follows. Or use the "Interview: My Friend" reproducible on page 100. Fill in the categories and use the information to write sentences. Talk as you compose each sentence.

Name	Age	Hair Color	Eye Color	Likes	Dislikes
(Tony)	(9)	(brown)	(brown)	(math, science, gym, soccer, baseball, computer games)	(spelling)

Supported Practice Afterward, you may want to give less experienced students a cloze paragraph such as the following to use as a warm-up activity before they write their own paragraphs.

67

My Friend _____

_____ is my friend. _____ is _____ years old. _____ has _____ hair and _____ eyes. He/She likes _____, _____, and _____. He/She doesn't like _____ or _____.

Rehearse Before Writing Allow students to rehearse what they want to write about by talking to a different partner. You might also copy and distribute the "Interview: My Friend" or the "What We Like About School" reproducibles on pages 100–101. Review the directions and have students complete the activities.

Writing Invite students to write about a friend or a class partner. Proficient students can work independently. Less experienced students may work with you in a small group. Once they finish, let them read what they've written to a partner for feedback. Encourage students to make additions or changes.

Student Self-assessments Create a chart such as the one that follows and distribute it to students. Use criteria that you emphasized during classwork. Have students complete self-assessments about their writing. Provide help as needed.

Did I begin my friend's name with a capital letter?	Yes	No
Did I use descriptive words? They are _____, _____, and _____.	Yes	No
Did I tell what my friend likes?	Yes	No
Did I tell what my friend dislikes?	Yes	No

Additional Reading

Calkins, Lucy McCormick. **The Art of Teaching Writing.** Heinemann, 1986.

Calkins, Lucy McCormick. **Writing Between the Lines.** Heinemann, 1991.

Graves, Donald H. **Writing: Teacher and Students at Work.** Heinemann, 1983.

Chapter 6

Integrating Language Learning in the Content Areas

Many students attain conversational proficiency in English within two years. The more demanding *academic* language proficiency, however, may take five to seven years or longer. How can we bridge the gap and facilitate students' language acquisition for academic purposes?

One of the best ways is to engage them in meaningful activities in the content areas. Students acquire language as they explore topics, interact with each other, and use language for a variety of purposes in the classroom.

An approach called the cognitive academic language learning approach, or CALLA, integrates academic language with content-based curriculum and learning strategies. It was developed to help upper elementary and secondary English-language learners succeed in science, math, and social studies (Chamot & O'Malley, 1990).

Graphic Organizers

Content areas require specialized vocabulary and academic language skills, such as sequencing, predicting, comparing, synthesizing, and evaluating. English-language learners will need extra support with these cognitively challenging tasks. Graphic organizers, Venn diagrams, graphs, and mind maps help students organize information to support the use of academic language.

Graphic organizers represent information in a visual pattern. They display the relationship between vocabulary and concepts. First, think of all the vocabulary items. Then decide on a way to organize the concepts. To help ESL students better grasp the relationships, use small sketches or drawings next to key words or concepts (similar to a rebus).

Demonstrate how to use graphic organizers step-by-step. Complete several examples of graphic organizers together before expecting students to work independently. Let students complete graphic organizers as they read a selection or listen to a video. Use graphic organizers to review concepts.

Matrices These are tables, charts, or grids that organize facts in several dimensions or categories. The example that follows organizes ocean life. The blank "Chart" reproducible on page 102 can be copied and distributed for students' use.

Ocean Life			
Animal	**Family**	**Body**	**Actions**
beluga whale	mammal	is warmblooded, is white	makes sounds like whistles and clicks
shark	fish	has scales, fins, tail	must swim or will sink

Star Graphs These represent examples or attributes of a given concept. Draw a circle or star with a central idea. Then draw radiating lines. On these lines, write key words and phrases that relate to the central idea. The example that follows describes attributes of a gorilla. The blank "Star Graph" reproducible on page 103 can be copied and distributed for students' use.

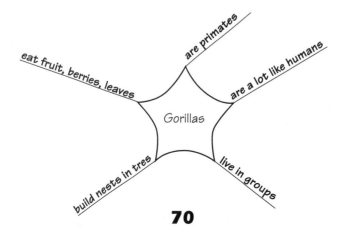

Webs   These link ideas to a central concept. A key word is written in the center, with lines drawn to related ideas. The blank "Web" reproducible on page 104 can be copied and distributed for students' use. (For an example of a web, see the web about culture on page 12.)

Venn Diagrams   Use these diagrams for comparing and contrasting two ideas. In the example that follows, the outer segments of the two circles show elements that are unique to schools in either country. The overlapping segment shows elements shared between schools in both countries. The blank "Venn Diagram" reproducible on page 105 can be copied and distributed for students' use.

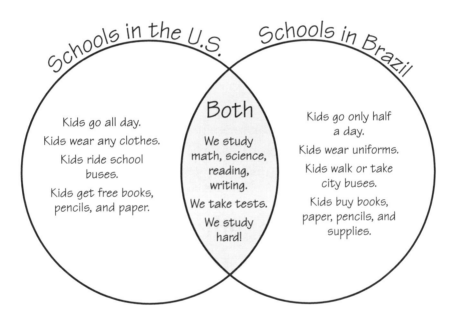

Mind Maps   These are nonlinear representations of a text, story, or presentation. The map can start anywhere on the page and branch outward. Use colors, drawings, and powerful key words to represent concepts and relationships (Buzan, 1989). Mind maps will vary because they show how a person visualizes concepts. The blank "Mind Map" reproducible on page 106 can be copied and distributed for students' use.

There are many creative ways to represent thinking and relationships between concepts. Examine magazines and newspapers for all the visual representations they offer. Adapt these whenever possible as aids for your English-language learners.

Putting It All Together: Theme Cycles

Theme cycles allow English-language learners to see the big picture and provide multiple opportunities to acquire language. The study is integrated across the curriculum, so content and concepts are visited from several perspectives.

As you design themes, be alert to opportunities to introduce new uses of language and to teach specific language skills within the context of the topic. You can incorporate ways to take students a step beyond their language level, challenging them to new learning.

Two theme cycles, Ocean Life and Celebrations, are described in this chapter. The needs of your students, the availability of resources, and your interests will shape the direction of the themes.

Ocean Life

The following suggestions are for a two- to three-week theme on ocean life. The time required to complete the activities is approximate. You will need materials on a variety of reading levels. You may need to adjust the theme according to student interest, grade level, and the availability of resources. Field trips and guest speakers give an extra dimension to the class study.

Day 1 Have students work in collaborative groups of mixed ability to brainstorm what they know about oceans. If possible, have students who are beginning English learners work with bilingual tutors to discuss what they know about oceans and ocean life.

Gather the class to learn what the small groups have identified. Make a class log or chart of their findings. Ask the class what they would like to know about ocean life, and chart their responses.

Review the chart periodically to evaluate statements. Can students identify inaccuracies as well as facts? Have they found answers to some of their questions?

Watch a video together or view a filmstrip about ocean life. Debrief the class through questions and answers, journal writing, labeling charts, and other follow-ups. Let ESL students watch portions of the video or the filmstrip again. If possible, you may also wish them to view it with a bilingual tutor.

Day 2 Display books, magazines, posters, and charts as reference materials for students to use while they explore the topic.

Set up a classroom display of seashells, coral, starfish, and other sea creatures. Enlist students' help in grouping the items. Show them how to use resource materials to label the display.

Have English-language learners begin a word bank of items related to the ocean theme. On one side of index cards they should write new words, and on the other they should add illustrations. Students can use their cards later during follow-up activities, such as putting the cards in categories or using them as references for reading and writing.

Day 3 Read sections from *Oceans* by Simon Seymour (Morrow Junior Books, 1990). The text is advanced, so you may wish to edit as you read, or use the pictures for a discussion. With the class, locate the major oceans of the world. What oceans are closest to your location? Has anyone seen the ocean?

Read aloud *Humphrey the Lost Whale* by Wendy Tokuda and Richard Hall (Heian International, 1986). Have students locate on a map where this true story took place. Show news clippings about scientists' efforts to rescue bottlenose whales and manatees. Discuss why these creatures are endangered. Invite students to write responses in their journals.

Day 4 Visit a local aquarium or pet shop that specializes in saltwater life. Prepare students for the field trip by reviewing the great variety of life forms that oceans sustain. Discuss what students might expect to see at the pet shop or aquarium. Generate a list of questions they might ask.

Day 5 Debrief the class about their trip. What did they see? What did they learn? Invite students to draw pictures about their field trip and write captions. Or have students create shape poems by using a favorite sea creature they saw on their trip.

To introduce shape poetry, take one of the items from the display table, such as a sand dollar, starfish, or shell. Draw its shape on chart paper. Inside the shape, write words and descriptive phrases related to the object.

You may also want to share published poems, such as Robert Froman's "The Beach" in *Poetry Power ESL* by Jeanne Piña and Katherine Maitland (Modern Curriculum Press, 1993). In this poem, words such as *waves* and *starfish* form their shapes. Ask students what other words they recognize.

Have students choose one of the sea animals they saw on the field trip. Let them brainstorm words about the animal. Then they should draw its shape and write the words inside the outline. More experienced students may want to draw a watery scene, such as an aquarium or a coral reef. Let them share their poems in small groups, then create a bulletin board to display the poetry.

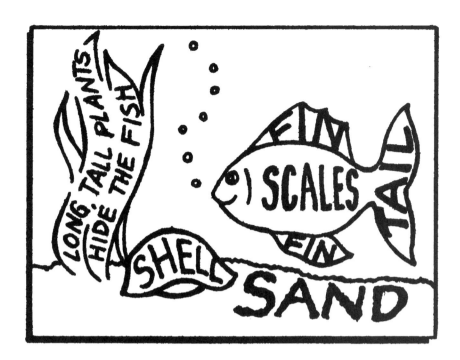

Day 6 Draw an imaginary sea creature and place it in a Mystery Box. Explain to students that you have been on a deep-sea dive and have found a new type of sea creature. Ask them to be scientists. What questions do they have about this mysterious creature? Lead them in generating questions and grouping these by categories.

Show them your sea creature and invite students to be reporters. Have them use the questions they generated to interview you.

Ask students to imagine they have discovered a new and mysterious sea creature. Invite them to use their imaginations in drawing and coloring one. Students then work with partners and take turns interviewing each other about their mysterious animals. Be sure to post the questions the class generated as a reference for less experienced students.

Days 7-8 Ask students to choose an intriguing ocean animal for further study. You may want to have them work on their projects with partners.

Distribute copies of the "Oceans Theme Report Guide" reproducible on page 107. Explain that it will help them sort and organize information. Walk them through the process of researching and note-taking.

Together, read about beluga whales or another topic of interest, and model how to jot down key words, phrases, and important concepts on the report guide. Have students use several sources to find the information. A completed report guide follows.

Report Guide

Name _____

Date _____

Animal: Beluga Whale

Where does it live?	What does it look like?
Arctic Ocean	adult: white, creamy color, 15 ft. long, weighs about 3,000 lb.; child: black or bluish, become white in about 5 years
What does it eat?	**Interesting Facts**
fish that live at the bottom of the sea	echolocation: sounds they make bounce off of plants, rocks, fish; use the noise to find fish to eat
How does it behave?	
travels in small family groups; makes strange noises like whistles, squeals, and clicks	

For fun, share Raffi's song "Baby Beluga" with the class (*Baby Beluga* by Raffi and D. Pike, Homeland Publishing, 1980). Write the words on a class chart and sweep your hands under the words as you sing. Compare information from the class research with information in the song. Are belugas portrayed accurately in the song? What other information might Raffi have sung about?

Tell students their research projects will take several days and you will help them in the process. You might allow groups to look for resources in the library. Others may view filmstrips, videos, or computer software. Work with small groups to guide them in using note-taking techniques. Help them use a variety of sources, such as magazines, books, and multimedia products.

Give students feedback as they complete their "Oceans Theme Report Guide." Have them return to their research to fill in the gaps as needed.

Day 9 Have students work with partners to compare and contrast their ocean animals. Be sure to model this process before you assign the work. For example, choose "shark" and "beluga whale." On a large piece of paper, draw a Venn diagram and label its parts. (See the information about beluga whales in the sample chart on page 76.)

Using information from the activity on Day 7, show students how to write notes on the diagram. Talk through the process and demonstrate how you think. After the demonstration, ask students to work with partners to compare and contrast their sea creatures. Distribute copies of the "Venn Diagram" reproducible on page 105. Students should use the information from their report guides to fill in the Venn diagram.

Days 10–12 Provide students with a variety of materials, such as clay, boxes, scraps of fabric, paints, and cardboard. Their assignment is to teach the class what they have learned by creating a display. Ask students to list five to ten questions that their display will answer. Then have them think of ways to represent the answers in their work. They may create illustrated posters, models of the animals, or dioramas.

Day 13 Give students time to rehearse their presentations. Encourage ESL students to tape their talks. Help them use the tape as feedback. Ask them how they can best share their message. Do they need to work on speed or intonation? Be sensitive to the needs of English learners. Students who are not ready to speak in front of the entire class may be able to share their projects with smaller groups or partners.

Related Literature

Adams, Georgie. **Fish Fish Fish.** Dial Books for Young Readers, 1994.

Baker, Lucy. **Life in the Oceans.** Scholastic, 1990.

Cole, Joanna. **Hungry, Hungry Sharks.** Random House, 1986.

Gibbons, Gail. **Sea Turtles.** Holiday House, 1995.

Gibbons, Gail. **Sharks.** Holiday House, 1992.

Gibbons, Gail. **Whales.** Holiday House, 1991.

Gribbin, Mary. **Big Ocean Creatures.** Ladybird Books, 1996.

Gruberson, Brenda. **Into the Sea.** Holt, 1996.

Himmelman, John. **Ibis.** Scholastic, 1990.

Hulme, Joy N. **Sea Squares.** Hyperion, 1991.

Hulme, Joy N. **Sea Sums.** Hyperion, 1996.

Métral, Yvette. **Animal World: The Dolphin.** Watermill Press, 1983.

Morris, Robert A. **Seahorse.** Harper & Row, 1972.

Pallotta, Jerry. **The Underwater Alphabet Book.** Charlesbridge, 1991.

Seymour, Simon. **Oceans.** Morrow Junior Books, 1990.

Swanson, Diane. **Safari Beneath the Sea.** Sierra Club for Students, 1994.

Tokuda, Wendy and Richard Hall. **Humphrey the Lost Whale.** Heian International, 1986.

Wax, Wendy and Della Rowland. **10 Things I Know About Whales.** Contemporary Books, 1990.

Teacher Resources

Ganer, Anita. **The Ocean Atlas.** Dorling Kindersley, 1994.

Piña, Jeanne and Katherine Maitland. "Way Down Deep" in **Poetry Power ESL.** Modern Curriculum Press, 1993.

Celebrations

The following suggestions can help you plan a two- to three-week theme cycle about celebrations that could be part of a larger unit about relationships. Students will study celebrations' similarities and differences in a variety of cultures. They will learn why people celebrate and on what occasions and how they celebrate important events.

Day 1 What special days can the class name? Brainstorm ideas about when people celebrate. Generate questions about what they want to understand about holidays and celebrations. List these to use later.

Read aloud *Fiesta! Cinco de Mayo* by June Behrens (Childrens Press, 1978). Discuss the main ideas by completing a chart such as the following. Using students' questions generated earlier, show the class how to organize important information.

Fiesta! by June Behrens

Celebration	Cinco de Mayo
When?	every 5th of May
Who?	Mexicans; Mexican Americans
Why?	On May 5, 1862, the Mexicans defeated the French.
What happens?	parties; traditional dances; Mexican food (tortillas, rice, beans); games (break piñatas)

Ask students to think of celebrations that they have experienced and choose one of these to share with the class. Together, discuss sources of information, including books, magazines, videos, and home resources. Have students look at their questions. What could they answer from personal experience and knowledge? What might their families answer?

Day 2 Model an oral report with a favorite holiday as the topic. Provide pictures of the celebration. Use props such as cards, decorations, music, or costumes. (Samples of special foods are a hit with students, too.)

Distribute copies of the "Celebrations Theme Research Guide" reproducible on page 108. Let students complete a chart while they listen to your report. Ask them to compare their chart with a partner's. Talk about important elements in the presentation. How do things like eye contact, posture, and speed of speaking affect the audience? On a chart, help students list ways to begin and end the reports. Make your own chart about your report to use later.

Review your expectations for oral reports. Highlight the most important questions students need to answer. Talk about how visual aids such as maps, pictures, or real objects add interest to the presentation. Distribute copies of the "Celebrations Theme: Planning My Oral Report" reproducible on page 109 to help them plan their presentation. Explain how to complete it.

Days 3-4 Let students conduct their research using library books, filmstrips, videos, magazines, and notes from family interviews. Have them organize their information, draw sketches, and prepare for their oral presentation.

Have students work with a partner to rehearse their report. Encourage them to tape their speech and review it for feedback. Take time to coach English learners. Provide encouragement and tips on vocabulary or organization.

Days 5-6 Distribute new copies of the "Celebrations Theme Research Guide" reproducible on page 108. Remind students how to complete it as they listen to each oral report. Videotape each presentation. As a follow-up, have the audience ask questions of the presenters.

Day 7 Let students watch the videotapes in small groups. Hand out copies of the "Audience Form" reproducible on page 110. Demonstrate how to give specific feedback, then have students do so by filling in the form. Hand out copies of the "How Well Did I Do?" reproducible on page 111. Have each complete a self-assessment of his or her presentation.

Day 8 Inform students that they will write a brief report about their celebration. All the writings will be clipped together in a book for them to take home.

Use the chart of main ideas about your favorite celebration to model how to write a short report on the subject. Emphasize answering the headings in the chart. Model how to create beginning and concluding remarks. Ask students to refer to their charts as they write a first draft about their celebration.

Day 9 Have students work with a partner to give each other feedback on their rough drafts. Is the beginning catchy and interesting? What information could they add to their report? Does the report have a good ending?

Work with individuals to give them feedback as well. Then have them revise their drafts and make illustrations to accompany their reports.

Day 10 Let students finish editing and completing their final draft. Copy the pages and have groups work to assemble the pages into a book for each class member. Encourage students to take their books home to share with their families. Keep several copies in your classroom library for future reference.

Related Literature

Adler, David. *A Picture Book of Hanukkah.* Holiday House, 1982.

Behrens, June. *Gung Hay Fat Choy.* Childrens Press, 1982.

Behrens, June. *Fiesta! Cinco de Mayo.* Childrens Press, 1978.

Gibbons, Gail. *Thanksgiving Day.* Holiday House, 1983.

Gibbons, Gail. *Christmas Time.* Holiday House, 1982.

Hayword, Linda. *The First Thanksgiving.* Random House, 1990.

Lowery, Linda. *Martin Luther King Day.* Carolrhoda, 1987.

Nerlove, Miriam. *Hanukkah.* Albert Whitman, 1989.

Pinkney, Andrea D. *Seven Candles for Kwanzaa.* Dial, 1993.

Porter, A.P. *Kwanzaa.* Carolrhoda, 1991.

Richecky, Janet. *Japanese Boy's Festival.* Childrens Press, 1994.

Waters, Kate and Madeline Slovenz-Low. *Lion Dancer.* Scholastic, 1990.

Teacher Resources

Piña, Jeanne and Maitland, Katherine. "Celebrations" in **Poetry Power ESL.** Modern Curriculum Press, 1993.

Polon, Linda and Aileen Cantwell. **The Whole Earth Holiday Book.** Scott, Foresman, 1983.

Silverthorne, Elizabeth. **Fiesta! Mexico's Great Celebrations.** Millbrook Press, 1992.

Theme Checklist

You may wish to use this checklist when you prepare your themes.

- Do I have a clear picture of the goal or learning outcome for this theme?

- Are the objectives for my students clearly defined? Do I know what I want to see from my students? (What will they be able to do and express that they couldn't before?)

- Have I planned activities across the curriculum? (math, science, language arts, social studies, music, art)

- Have I taken students' cultures into account? Are there opportunities to tap into cross-cultural learning?

- Have I provided ways for students to use their home language?

- Have I developed activities to tap students' prior knowledge?

- Do I have pictures, charts, realia, and so on, to bridge the gap between language and understanding concepts?

- Are there reading materials on a broad range of levels, from easy to advanced?

- Did I plan for opportunities in the four skill areas: listening, speaking, reading, and writing? Do these activities include individual, small-group, and whole-class formats?

- Are there activities that allow students to demonstrate learning through modes that are not dependent on language, such as art, movement, or music?

Chapter 7

A Final Word

Working with English-language learners is a challenge and a privilege. Students bring a rich background of world views and cultural experiences to our classrooms. We can glimpse different ways of life from these students and their families. Through them, we can travel the world and learn about other cultures. By living and working with them, we renew our understanding of ourselves. Our capacity for compassion, kindness, and empathy cuts across cultural barriers.

Schools need to invite students to use their backgrounds to forge connections and construct meaning. English-language learners must make connections from the known to the unknown; from family life to school life; and from home language to the English language.

Our classrooms must help students make these connections. We can do this by providing opportunities for students to engage in social interactions:

- to ask questions and solve problems;

- to explore theme cycles, revisiting a topic from several perspectives;

- to use language for meaningful purposes, such as asking for information, relating personal experiences, comparing and contrasting, describing, and evaluating.

Shy students like Yuki need to be encouraged to reach beyond their comfort level and forge friendships with American students.

Students like Hima, with gaps in their cultural awareness, benefit from becoming familiar with aspects we take for granted, such as traditional literature from Western culture. They also need opportunities to share their rich cultural experiences.

Daniel exemplifies the student who fits in quickly and develops strong decoding skills, but fails to understand what he reads. Students like Daniel need to learn comprehension strategies.

Felipe appears to be a proficient English speaker. He chats with friends, answers questions, and "gets along." However, he is in trouble academically. Some teachers see students like Felipe as stubborn, belligerent, or even "slow." We should view such students as having acquired basic social skills in English, but needing an environment that will foster the acquisition of "school language."

Helping English-language learners succeed in school is our challenge. We can help students cross cultures by connecting home life with school. We can create an environment that not only accepts but promotes students' primary languages. We can help them acquire English by ensuring that they have lots of comprehensible input and by providing opportunities for them to interact in meaningful ways.

In so doing, we will foster an environment that invites students to add English to their lives. And maybe in the process, we will find that *we* have gained rich experiences that make it all worthwhile.

References

• • • Introduction • • •

Fillmore, L.W. "When Learning a Second Language Means Losing the First." **Early Childhood Research Quarterly,** 6, 1991, 323–346.

"NCBE Responds to Frequently Asked Questions." NCBE **(National Clearinghouse for Bilingual Education)** Forum, XVI, No. 3, March 1993, 1, 4–5.

"The Changing Face of American Schools." **NCBE Forum,** XVIII, No. 4, Fall 1995, 1, 5–7.

Liu, Eric. "Why We Need Immigrants." **USA Weekend,** September 23–25, 1994, 4–6.

Jones, Rachel. "Hispanic Kids in a Box," **Detroit Free Press,** July 2, 1996, 8a.

Development Associates. "Summary of Bilingual Education: State Educational Agency Program Survey of States' Limited English Proficient Persons and Available Educational Services 1993–1994." **NCBE**, September 27, 1995.

• • • Chapter 1 • • •
Second-Language Acquisition

Cummins, J. **Bilingualism and Special Education: Issues in Assessment and Pedagogy**. Multilingual Matters, 1984.

Dulay, H., M. Burt, and S. Krashen. **Language Two.** Oxford University Press, 1982, 3–71.

Freeman, D. and Y. Freeman. **Between Worlds: Access to Second Language Acquisition.** Heinemann, 1994, 67–107.

Krashen, S. **The Input Hypothesis: Issues and Implications.** Longman, 1985.

What Affects Language Acquisition?

Brown, H.D. *Principles of Language Learning and Teaching* (2nd ed.). Prentice-Hall, 1987, 78–143.

Clayton, Jacklyn Blake. *Your Land, My Land: Students in the Process of Acculturation.* Heinemann, 1996.

Collier, V.P. "Age and Rate of Acquisition of Second Language for Academic Purposes." *TESOL (Teachers of English to Speakers of Other Languages) Quarterly,* 21(3), December 1987.

Collier, V.P. "Acquiring a Second Language for School." *Directions in Language & Education* 1(4), NCBE, Fall 1995.

Dulay, H., M. Burt, M. and S. Krashen. *Language Two.* Oxford University Press, 1982, 34–95.

Willet, J. "Becoming First Graders in an L2: An Ethnographic Study of L2 Socialization." *TESOL Quarterly,* 29(3), Autumn 1995.

The Role of Culture

Althen, Gary. *American Ways: A Guide for Foreigners in the United States.* Intercultural Press, 1988.

Clayton, Jacklyn Blake. *Your Land, My Land: Students in the Process of Acculturation.* Heinemann, 1996.

Dima, Nicholas. *Cross-Cultural Communication.* Institute for the Study of Man, 1990.

Hall, Edward T. *Beyond Culture.* Anchor Press/Doubleday, 1976.

Hall, Edward T. *The Silent Language.* Doubleday, 1959.

Hull, J.D. "The State of the Union," *Time,* January 1995, 52–75.

Kohls, L.R. *Survival Kit for Overseas Living* (3rd. ed.). Intercultural Press, 1996.

• • • Chapter 2 • • •
Helping Students Add English

First Days

Cummins, J. "The Role of Primary Language Development in Promoting Educational Success for Language Minority Students." *Schooling and Language Minority Students: A Theoretical Framework,* Evaluation, Dissemination and Assessment Center, School of Education, California State University, 1981.

Cummins, J. *Bilingualism and Special Education: Issues in Assessment and Pedagogy.* Multilingual Matters, 1984.

Freeman, D. and Y. Freeman. "Ten Tips for Monolingual Teachers of Bilingual Students." *Whole Language for Second Language Learners,* Heinemann, 1992.

Hudelson, S. "The Role of Native Language Literacy in the Education of Language Minority Students. *Language Arts,* 64(8), December 1987, 827–841.

Classroom Techniques

Enright, S. "Use Everything You Have to Teach English: Providing Useful Input to Young Language Learners." *Students and ESL Integrating Perspectives* edited by P. Rigg and S. Enright, TESOL, 1986, 115–162.

Freeman, D.E. and Y.S. Freeman. *Between Worlds: Access to Second Language Acquisition.* Heinemann, 1994.

Krashen, S.D. *The Input Hypothesis: Issues and Implications.* Longman, 1985.

Smith, F. *Joining the Literacy Club: Selected Paper and Some Afterthoughts.* Heinemann, 1983.

Wong-Fillmore, L. "When Does Teacher Talk Work as Input?" *Input in Second Language Acquisition* edited by S.M. Gass and C.G. Madden, Newbury House, 1985, 17–50.

• • • Chapter 3 • • •
Listening and Speaking

Asher, J. *Learning Another Language Through Actions: The Complete Teacher's Guidebook* (3rd ed.). Sky Oaks Productions, 1988.

Dulay, H., M. Burt and S. Krashen. *Language Two.* Oxford University Press, 1982, 13–44.

Enright, D.S. and M.L. McCloskey. "Providing Real Oral Discourse." *Integrating English: Developing English Language and Literacy in the Multilingual Classroom,* Addison-Wesley, 1988, 123–163.

Krashen, S.D. and T.D. Terrell. *The Natural Approach.* The Alemany Press, 1983.

Omaggio, A. *Teaching Language in Context.* Heinle & Heinle, 1986, 121–173.

Seely, C. and E. Romijn. *TPR Is More than Commands—At All Levels.* Command Performance Language Institute, 1995.

Segal, B. *Teaching English as a Second Language Part II: Speaking, Reading, Writing.* Berty Segal, (date unknown), 4–23.

Ur, P. *Teaching Listening Comprehension.* Cambridge University Press, 1984.

• • • Chapter 4 • • •
Reading

Ashton-Warner, S. *Teacher.* Simon & Schuster, 1963.

Allen, V.F. *Techniques in Teaching Vocabulary.* Oxford University Press, 1983.

Cazden, C.B. *Classroom Discourse: The Language of Teaching and Learning.* Heinemann, 1988.

Cummins, J. "The Role of Primary Language Development in Promoting Educational Success for Language Minority Students." *Schooling and Language Minority Students: A Theoretical Framework,* Evaluation, Dissemination and Assessment Center, School of Education, California State University, 1981.

Enright, D.S. and M.L. McCloskey. "Providing Real Written Discourse." *Integrating English: Developing English Language and Literacy in the Multilingual Classroom,* Addison-Wesley, 1988, 165–203.

Hamayan, E. and M. Pfleger. *"Developing Literacy in English as a Second Language: Guidelines for Teachers of Young Students from Non-literate Backgrounds."* **NCBE,** September 1987.

Holmes, B.C. and N.L. Roser. "Five Ways to Assess Readers' Prior Knowledge." **The Reading Teacher,** March 1987, 646–649.

Hudelson, S. "Kan Yu Ret an Rayt en Ingles: Students Become Literate in English as a Second Language." **TESOL Quarterly** 18(2), June 1984, 221–237.

Rigg, P. "Reading in ESL: Learning from Kids." **Students and ESL: Integrating Perspectives** edited by P. Rigg and S.D. Enright, TESOL, 1986, 55–91.

Smith, Frank. **Essays into Literacy.** Heinemann, 1983.

• • • Chapter 5 • • •
Writing

Berlitz, C. **Native Tongues.** Putnam, 1982.

Cambourne, B. "Process Writing and Non-English Speaking Background Students." **Australian Journal of Reading,** 9(3), August 1986, 126–138.

Enright, D.S. and M.L. McCloskey. "Providing Real Written Discourse." **Integrating English: Developing English Language and Literacy in the Multilingual Classroom,** Addison-Wesley, 1988, 165–203.

Hudelson, S. "Kan Yu Ret an Rayt en Ingles: Students Become Literate in English as a Second Language." **TESOL Quarterly** 18(2), June 1984, 221–237.

Hudelson, S. "ESL Students' Writing: What We've Learned, What We're Learning." **Students and ESL: Integrating Perspectives** edited by P. Rigg and D.S. Enright, TESOL, 1986, 23–54.

Kreeft, J. "Dialogue Writing: Bridge from Talk to Essay Writing." **Language Arts** 61(2), February 1984, 141–150.

• • • Chapter 6 • • •
Integrating Language Learning in the Content Areas

Buzan, T. *Use Both Sides of Your Brain.* New York: Penguin Books, 1989.

Chamot, A.U. and J.M. O'Malley. *Learning Strategies in Second Language Acquisition.* Cambridge University Press, 1990.

Hyerle, D. "Thinking Maps: Seeing Is Understanding." *Educational Leadership* 53(4), December 1995, January 1996, 85–89.

Johnson, L.L. "Learning Across the Curriculum with Creative Graphing." *Journal of Reading* 32(6), March 1989, 509–19.

Wood, K.D. and J.A. Mateja. "Adapting Secondary Level Strategies for Use in Elementary Classrooms." *The Reading Teacher* 36(6), February 1983, 492–96.

Reproducibles

Bingo Grid

Name _____

Date _____

		FREE SPACE		

Tell a Story

Draw pictures to tell your story.

Name _____

Date _____

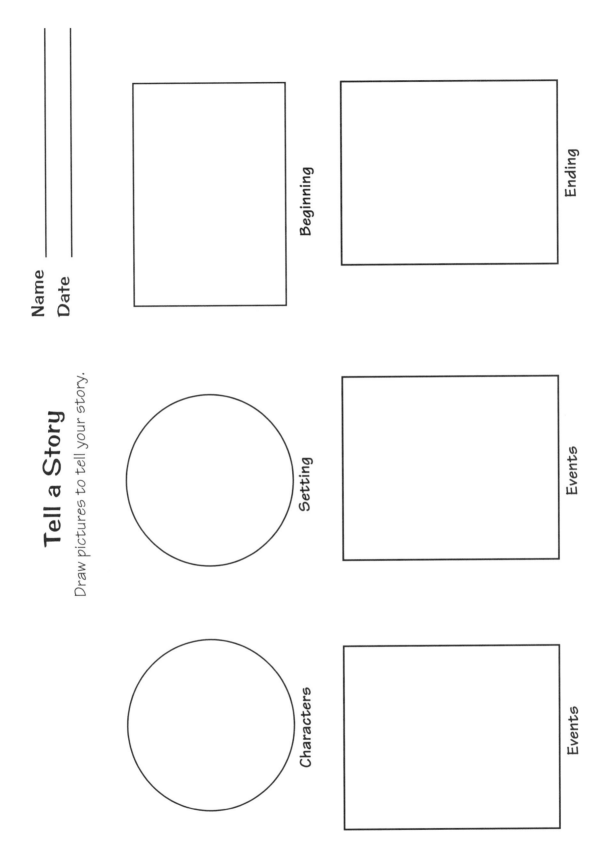

Characters

Setting

Beginning

Events

Events

Ending

Survey I

Name _____

Date _____

Write a question to ask your classmates.

Question: _____

_____

Name	Answer
1.	
2.	
3.	
4.	
5.	
6.	
7.	
8.	
9.	
10.	

Survey 2

Name _____

Date _____

Write or draw three choices in the boxes below. Make an **X** to show your classmates' answers.

Question: Which do you like best?

Name			
1.			
2.			
3.			
4.			
5.			
6.			
7.			
8.			
9.			
10.			
11.			
12.			

Survey 3

Name _____

Date _____

Think of two things you want to compare. Write a word or draw a picture for the **first** item in both boxes labeled 1. Write a word or draw a picture for the **second** item in both boxes labeled 2.

Interview classmates to find out which item they like better. Tally their answers next to the correct item.

Example: Which do you like better, ⚽ or 🏀 ?

Which do you like better?

	or	
Box 1		Box 2

Tallies

Box 1

Tallies

Box 2

Calendar Grid

Name _____

Date _____

Write the name of the month. Fill in the days in the correct boxes. Draw pictures to show the holidays.

Month: _____

Sunday	Monday	Tuesday	Wednesday	Thursday	Friday	Saturday

Writing Plan

Name _____

Date _____

Circle or write your answer.

What am I writing?

letter 　　　postcard 　　　story

book 　　　message 　　　other

Who will read what I write?

teacher 　　　friend

class 　　　family

principal 　　　?

Letter Form

_____
(date)

Dear _____
(greeting)

_____

_____

_____

_____

_____

_____

_____

_____

_____

_____
(closing)

_____
(your name)

Interview: My Friend

Name _____

Date _____

My Friend _____
(name)

Complete the chart with information about your friend.

Last Name	
Age	
Hair	
Eyes	
Brothers/Sisters	
Likes	
Dislikes	

What We Like About School

Name_____

Date _____

Friend_____

Talk with your friend about school.

1. Write things that *you like* but your friend *doesn't like* in the outer left circle.

2. Write things that *your friend likes* but you *don't like* in the outer right circle.

3. Write things *you both like* in the middle.

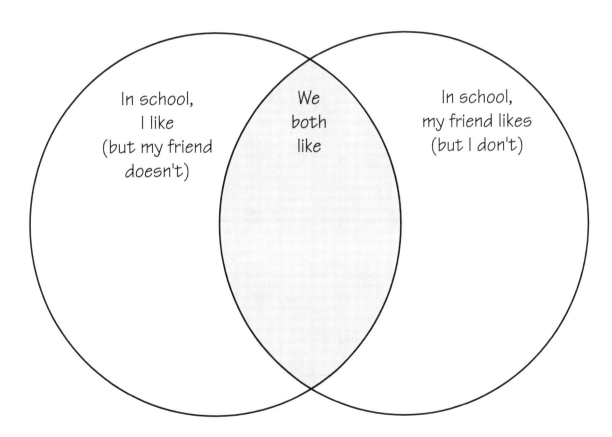

In school,
I like
(but my friend
doesn't)

We
both
like

In school,
my friend likes
(but I don't)

Name _____

Date _____

Chart

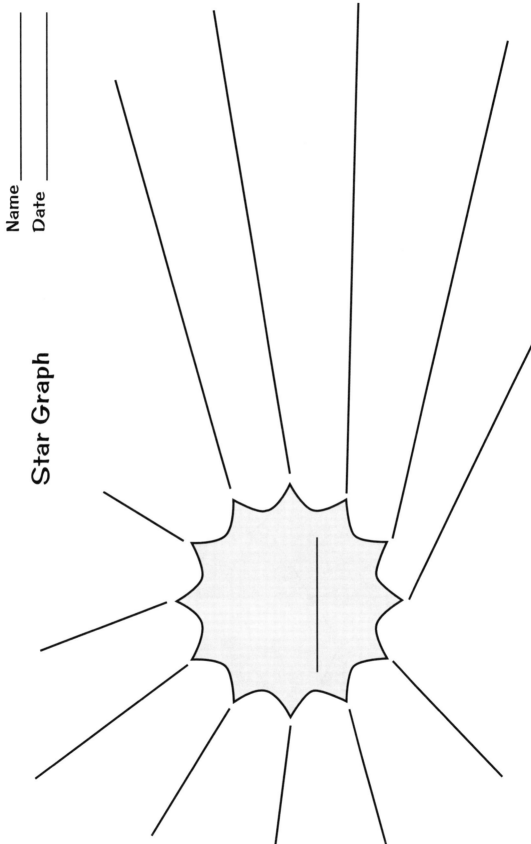

Name _____

Date _____

Star Graph

Web

Venn Diagram

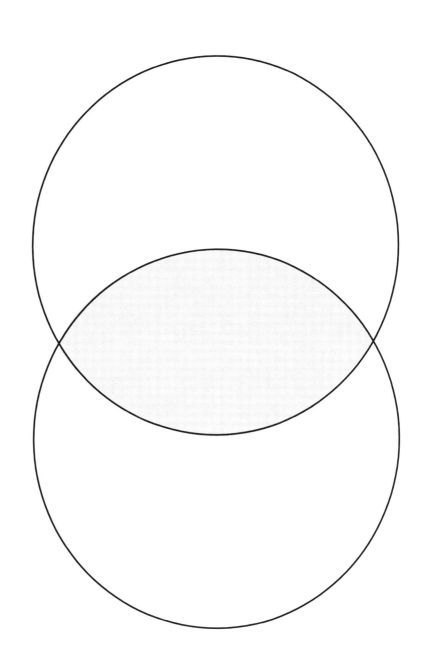

Mind Map

Name_____

Date _____

What is your topic?_____

Write it somewhere on the page.

Use pictures, colors, and words to tell more about your topic.
Be creative!

Oceans Theme
Report Guide

Name _____

Date _____

Animal _____

Where does it live?	What does it look like?
What does it eat?	**Interesting Facts**
How does it behave?	

Celebrations Theme
Research Guide

Name _____

Date _____

Celebration	
Time of Year	
Who Celebrates?	
Why?	
Special Clothing	
Special Foods	
Special Place	
What Do People Do?	

Celebrations Theme
Planning My Oral Report

Name_____

Date _____

Celebration_____

Country _____

I will use:

☐ a map   ☐ objects

☐ pictures   ☐ music

☐ chart   ☐ other

Questions to ask my family:

1. _____

   _____

2. _____

   _____

3. _____

   _____

4. _____

   _____

Celebrations Theme: Oral Report
Audience Form

Name _____

Date _____

Speaker's Name _____

1. Did the speaker look at the audience?

    not at all   some of the time   most of the time

<———>

2. How did the speaker talk?

    too slow   just right   too fast

<———>

3. Did the speaker use things to tell the story?

maps   music

charts   objects

pictures

other _____

4. Did the speaker have a good beginning to the report?

   Yes   No

5. Did the speaker have an interesting ending to the report?

   Yes   No

Celebrations Theme: Oral Report
How Well Did I Do?

Name _____

Date _____

1. I looked at the audience.

    never   some of the time   most of the time

<-->

2. I spoke directly to the audience.

    never   some of the time   most of the time

<-->

3. I used these things to tell my story:

maps   music

charts   objects

pictures

other   _____

4. I had a good beginning to my report.

      Yes   No

5. I had an interesting ending to my report.

      Yes   No

Teacher Resources

Lipson, Eden Ross. *Parent's Guide to the Best Books for Students.* Times Books, 1988.

Piña, Jeanne and Katherine Maitland. *Poetry Power ESL.* Modern Curriculum Press, 1993.

Raines, Shirley C. and Robert J. Canady. *Story S-T-R-E-T-C-H-E-R-S: Activities to Expand Children's Favorite Books.* Gryphon House, 1989.

Routman, Regie. *Invitations.* Heinemann, 1991.

Smallwood, Betty Ansin. *The Literature Connection: A Read-Aloud Guide for Multicultural Classrooms.* Addison-Wesley, 1991.

Thiessen, Diane and Margaret Matthias (eds.). *The Wonderful World of Mathematics: A Critically Annotated List of Children's Books in Mathematics.* The National Council of Teachers of Mathematics, 1992.

Welchman-Tischler, Rosamond. *How to Use Children's Literature to Teach Mathematics.* The National Council of Teachers of Mathematics, 1992.